ADVENTURE IN DYING

ADVENTURE IN DYING

By

NANCY KARO

with

ALVERA MICKELSEN

MOODY PRESS
CHICAGO

Except where indicated otherwise, all direct quotations of Scripture are taken from the New American Standard Bible, © 1960, 1962, 1963, 1971, and 1973 by The Lockman Foundation, and are used by permission.

The use of selected references from various versions of the Bible in this publication does not necessarily imply publisher endorsement of the versions in their entirety.

Library of Congress Cataloging in Publication Data

Karo, Nancy
Adventure in dying.

1. Apostles' Creed—Sermons. 2. Baptists—Sermons. 3. Sermons, American. 4. Cancer—Personal narratives. 5. Karo, Lindon. I. Mickelsen, Alvera, joint author. II. Title.

BT993.2.K37 242'.4 76-809

ISBN 0-8024-0141-4

Printed in the United States of America

To

our three sons:

Steve,

Rob,

Scott

Contents

Foreword

"DEATH AT A YOUNG AGE seems tragic to us now, but from the vantage point of a hundred years hence—or from eternity—we'll realize that it is not how *long* we live but how *well* we live that matters." My father said that to me in January 1973, a few months before Lindon Karo died. At that time it was hard for me to accept the truth of what he said. I was wrestling intensely with God in prayer that He would heal Lindon.

When God did not heal him, it took several months before I could focus properly on how *well* Lindon had lived. At first there was only the deep grief over his death. But continued struggle, time, prayer, and fellowship provided the refocusing I needed. In June, three months after his death, I was able to preach at Salem Baptist Church on the simple theme, "God is great and God is good," and apply it to the life and death of Lindon Karo.

God was good in allowing us to have Lindon as long as we did. During those days, our lives were deeply affected by how well he lived.

He loved life right to the end. That love arose from his experience with God, an experience that included his probing mind, his human sensitivity, his excitement over preaching, and his discovery of the four new relationships possible in God's Kingdom: with God, with self, with others who are significant, with the world.

As I read the manuscript of Nancy's book, I wept as I recalled his times of great suffering. These involved not only physical pain, but also the pain of knowing he would not live to rear his three sons or to pastor Salem church or to grow old with his wife.

One day as we were having lunch together during his remission in September, he shared some of his feelings about Nancy. "She is just a great gal," he said. "I just can't get over how good she is for me."

We are grateful that she has been willing to relive these painful days as she has told the story of the last months of Lindon's life. She has helped us to see clearly that it is not how long we live but how well we live that matters.

LELAND V. ELIASON
Director of Field Education
Bethel Theological Seminary

Preface

THERE HAVE BEEN TIMES when I did not want to write this book. The pain of losing my husband was so poignant that I thought I would just like to live through my grief, experience God's healing with time, and then go on following Lin's frequent advice: "Don't look back."

But I could not for two reasons. First, God had taught me so much during those painful months that I felt impelled to share it any way I could. I had learned what it means to live in the midst of a ministering community that included our church, relatives, friends, and many Christians spread around the world. God not only held my hand, He also sent many of His children to hold my hand, to pray, to encourage, to weep with us. (And also to clean our house, do my ironing, and paint the house!) Those children of God included not only mature Christians who had lived through the loss of loved ones, but it included teenagers and even small children who smiled up into my eyes Sunday after Sunday, or squeezed my hand, or wrote scrawling notes to Lin and me. This is really a love story, and true love is always a dynamic, expanding force that changes whomever it touches. Lin realized this keenly. And just a few days before his death he told Lee Eliason, "Keep Nancy sharing. The Word means so much to her."

But there is a second reason for this book. Lin wanted to write it. From November 1972 until his death in March

1973, he thought and struggled to make it a reality. He talked a lot about sharing his adventure in dying. He wrote a few pages in November and always intended to get on with it as soon as he felt better. He never recovered enough to write the book. During the last few months he had one aim in mind: he wanted to preach as much as possible. He firmly believed in the ministry of preaching. He was convinced that what he said on Sunday mornings could and did make a difference in people's lives.

He had planned a series on the Apostles' Creed for several months. His diagnosis of cancer came just before he was to begin the series.

Although he talked freely about his illness in his sermons, it was never a dominant theme. He always wanted the minds of people directed toward his great God and the love He had shown toward all of us. And so the sermons reveal the truths that to him were the most important, even when he was dying of cancer. The sermons were all taped, and a month after his death I began transcribing the tapes. The condensations of those last sermons appear as part of this book.

God's children not only stood with us in encouragement and prayer during Lin's illness and death, but they have stood with me in the writing of this book. They include members of Salem Baptist Church, New Brighton, Minnesota, where Lin was pastor until his death; friends; neighbors; my father and mother, Lloyd and Shirley Russell, who have made helping us their major task; and my sister, Judy Ferrin, in Phoenix, who has encouraged me via the telephone these many months. The staff at St. Paul Ramsey Hospital was helpful in furnishing medical records.

My friend Alvera Mickelsen helped me with the actual writing of the book. I was having a bad time until she said to me, "Talk into a tape recorder everything you can remember. Then type it all up, and I'll try to help you make it interesting." She spent many hours revising and editing the manuscript.

My hope is that these pages will help the reader to know the strength and comfort God can give us. He meets us in our weakness and imparts His strength, His courage. He wraps us around with love when our security and life seem tumbling down. He is God the Father Almighty, Maker of heaven and earth.

The Apostles' Creed

I believe in God the Father Almighty,
Maker of heaven and earth.
And in Jesus Christ, His only Son, our Lord,
who was conceived by the Holy Ghost,
born of the Virgin Mary,
suffered under Pontius Pilate,
was crucified, dead and buried;
He descended into hell;
the third day He rose again from the dead;
He ascended into heaven, and sitteth on the right hand of God the Father Almighty;
from thence He shall come to judge the quick and the dead.
I believe in the Holy Ghost,
the holy catholic church,
the communion of saints,
the forgiveness of sins,
the resurrection of the body,
and the life everlasting.

Amen.

1
Tiptoe in Expectancy

THE SUMMER of 1972 seemed so promising. My husband, Lindon, had come to pastor Salem Baptist Church, New Brighton, Minnesota, the year before, and now everything seemed to say "All Systems Go." It was a middle-class suburban church about three miles from Bethel College and Theological Seminary from which Lindon had graduated in 1966 and 1969. The church was only nine years old with a membership of 170, but it was alive and open to the kind of leadership that Lin had to offer. The new sanctuary, seating about 450, was just being completed. Much of the finishing work was being done by volunteer labor, and Lin had spent many evenings and Saturdays pounding, sanding, and sawing with the other men. He loved the camaraderie and fellowship that grew out of those hours working together.

Our three young boys were healthy and happy. I had taken an office job in the spring to help clear up some debts we had before we came to the church. We had the usual kinds of problems for young families, but we had a sense of destiny and God's call to His service that made us greet each day with eagerness.

The church itself was growing rapidly. Many new families were coming, and some were finding Christ. The church was blessed with exceptionally good lay leadership that made it easy for Lin to concentrate on his first love: preaching.

One day during the summer of 1972, as Lin played tennis with one of the men of the church, he shared his eager expectation of the future and said, "This year has been the best year of my life."

Our lives had not always fallen into such pleasant places, especially for Lin. His parents had divorced when he was five years old. During the following years his mother had remarried and moved several times. By the time he entered high school he had become lonely and fearful and had learned to repress his feelings so that the hurts would not show. But during his sophomore year in high school, a chum introduced him to Jesus Christ, and everything began to change. He began to see people in the light of God's love, and life took on meaning and purpose.

After high school he enlisted for two years in the Evangelism Corps, sponsored by the Baptist General Conference. The group was composed of young people who volunteered to give one or two years of their lives to various kinds of evangelism, mostly door-to-door visiting under the auspices of sponsoring churches.

It was during these years in the Evangelism Corps that we became acquainted. I, too, had joined the group for the years 1959 and 1960. When our term of service was completed, we married and set up housekeeping in Santa Maria, California, where Lin worked at Boeing Aircraft and I worked as a secretary. Already Lin had his sights set toward Bethel College. We saved every cent possible, and in 1963 we moved to Minnesota where he began college. I took an office job again, and he secured part-time work as a youth pastor at Minnetonka Baptist Church. He studied and studied and studied. During this period two of our sons were born: Steve in 1962 and Rob in 1965. When Lin graduated from Bethel College in 1966, he immediately enrolled in Bethel Seminary. That meant three more years of study and work and study and work.

We were very thankful for a call to Spring Vale Baptist Church near Cambridge, Minnesota. The church had a parsonage to which we moved. Lin served as full-time pastor and full-time student. It was a grueling schedule, but Lin was physically and psychologically robust. He found his recreation in sports, and he excelled in baseball, golf, handball, tennis, and swimming. In 1969 he graduated from the seminary as valedictorian.

In 1969 we moved to Altadena Baptist Church, California. We loved Altadena. Furthermore, my parents lived out there, and so did Lin's mother and sister. But when the call came from Salem in New Brighton, we felt led of God to accept it, and all that had happened since we came seemed to verify that God had a special ministry for us here.

Little did we dream what that ministry included.

2

Ominous Clouds

On Saturday, August 5, Lin went to Trout Lake Camp to serve as a teacher for senior high young people. When he got there, he wrote in his diary that he had pain in the middle of his chest. He tried to ignore it, thinking it was simply gas.

He was in pain the entire week, but he maintained his schedule of activities and enjoyed his teaching sessions with the young people. He returned home late Friday night. When he woke on Saturday with the same nagging pain, he called Dr. Carl Christenson, one of our parishioners. Chris prescribed some pain pills and suggested that he go to the hospital for a checkup. Lin felt that, perhaps when the weekend was over, he would do that if he did not feel better.

On that Saturday night, Dr. and Mrs. Paul Patterson, other parishioners, had invited us to a Viking football game and tailgate dinner (eating in the parking lot before the game). Lin wanted to go so much—he was an avid sports fan—that he was sure he would perk up and feel OK when he got there. However, he did not feel like eating; and when we went inside the stadium, he complained of feeling faint. He and Paul went under the stadium and sat down. Lin said, "I just want to lie down and go to sleep." Then he vomited and after that felt better, although his pain continued throughout the game. Dr. Patterson, an orthopedic surgeon, was deeply concerned and felt there could be something seriously the matter.

By the time we went home he knew he felt too sick to preach the next morning; but he did not feel he could get anyone in his place at such short notice, so he determined to go ahead. He did not feel he could say he was too sick to preach when he had gone to the football game the night before!

He did preach the next morning, hanging onto the pulpit for support. This was in sharp contrast to his usual style of walking around the wide platform.

As soon as we got home from church, I asked Dr. Christenson to come over and look at him. He did so and immediately called St. Paul Ramsey Hospital, where he was in a specialist residency, to arrange for Lin's checking in.

When Lin arrived at the hospital, x rays were taken and a heart specialist called in. First indications pointed to much fluid in the left lung, and a mass around the heart that could be due to a blood clot or a tumor.

On Monday a full range of tests began. When I finished work on Monday afternoon, I went to see Lin at the hospital. He tried to tell me gently that the doctors suspected Hodgkin's disease, a cancer of the lymph glands; and, for the first time in my life, I saw Lin cry. I was taken aback, but I was glad that in this time of great stress he could release his feelings in this way. In the months ahead, I would see that his growing ability and willingness to express his feelings would be of help to himself, to me, and to our church. But at that darkest moment in our eleven years of marriage, we just clung to each other and wept together. In my shock, I held onto the hope that the diagnosis was wrong. A bone-marrow test was scheduled for Tuesday and a biopsy for Wednesday to determine just what the mass was in his chest. We never imagined they would find something *worse* than Hodgkin's.

Tuesday evening I left the boys with neighbors so I could visit Lin. When I arrived, Ralph and Nancy Cullen from church and two other couples were there. Lin told me that the doctor wanted to talk with us alone, so the visitors stepped out and the young intern came in.

He simply announced that Lin had lymphosarcoma. We had never heard the word before but the ending of it, "sarcoma," had an ominous sound. His explanation was businesslike: "Worse than Hodgkin's disease, but better than leukemia."

I looked at him unbelieving. Was he trying to tell us that Lindon had *cancer*? He said there was a tumor the size of a baseball in Lin's chest. "And I won't say it is benign. Do you have any questions?"

Questions! How do you ask questions when your mind is in turmoil? Two weeks ago Lin had seemed vigorous and healthy, a thirty-one-year-old man at the peak of physical prowess. Was he now saying that Lin would die? Or be permanently hospitalized? Was he through as a pastor?

We finally collected ourselves enough to ask a few questions and how they would treat this disease. The young intern told what he knew about the disease but said he didn't know the treatment. However, he assured us they would start something. After the doctor left, we sat looking at each other. We were so shocked we barely knew what to say.

Finally I knew I had to go back out to the waiting room and invite the visitors back. We walked back to the room together, and Lindon told them calmly. He recounted nearly everything the doctor had said to us: that lymphosarcoma is a rare cancer with only about one hundred cases a year in the United States. Then Lin led in prayer, and he was able to thank God for His goodness. The visitors excused themselves so that we could have some time alone.

Later that same evening, Gordon Lindquist, a layman from Salem church, came to see Lin. He had been out of town for the weekend and had just returned to learn that Lin was in the hospital. He had called Dr. Christenson, and Carl had laid out the brutal medical facts for him, warning him that Lin and I had not yet been told but would be that evening.

Gordy walked in about 8:30 that evening, tears streaming down his face. He held out his arms and hugged Lin. It was a deeply meaningful moment, and they wept freely together.

I later learned that on that same Tuesday evening, Dr. Christenson was meeting with members of the Salem church board, telling them the medical facts and the probable course of the disease. Their shock was like ours. They agreed to notify every member to come to an all-church prayer meeting the next evening where the pastor's illness would be discussed.

When I left the hospital that night, I could hardly see to drive home. I could only cry, "Help, God! Help!" Questions pounded at me. What would I do? How could I tell our boys? I had to stop at the Robert Kendalls where our three sons—Steve, nine; Rob, seven; and Scotty, two and one-half—had been staying while I went to the hospital. I was under control when I reached there; but when I tried to tell Bob and Marilyn the doctor's verdict, I fell apart again. Since it was summer vacation, some friends offered to take Steve and Scotty up to their farm near Cambridge forty miles away. My next-door neighbor offered to take Rob for the next few days, for she had a son the same age.

But before the boys left, I had to try to tell them what was happening. Scotty was too young to understand anything except that he wanted Daddy to come home. Rob sat bewildered, waiting for Steve to ask the inevitable question: "Will Dad die?" I explained the little that I knew—that the doctors would try the drugs and treatment that was available, and that God could heal if He so chose. We would pray for that.

That night, with no one else in the house, I tried to sort things out in my mind. I read on in 1 Samuel, where I had been reading for my devotional time. In 1 Samuel 12:16 I read, "Stand still and see the great wonders which the LORD will do before your eyes" (NEB*). I didn't know what the wonder would be. I hoped desperately that it would be Lin's healing; but whatever it was to be, God would be there. Then in verse 24, I read, "Consider what great things He has done for you." God had already done many great things in our lives, and I knew that now, when I needed Him so much, God was there.

After I left the hospital that night, other visitors had come, the Reverend Emmett Johnson, director of the Minnesota Baptist Conference, and the Reverend Frank Voth, pastor of nearby Spring Lake Park Church. They had learned from Carl Christenson about the seriousness of the illness. Lin looked at them and said, "Well, I guess you've heard the news." Emmett responded, "Yes." Emmett later recounted his amazement at the positive outlook Lindon had. "We'll work from here," Lindon had said. "I'm planning to make it."

But, after they left, Lin later recorded that he had a night of intense struggle. It was not fear, but great confusion. He felt that his plans and vision had been of God. He had looked forward so long and worked so hard on his coming sermons on the Apostles' Creed. He had many ideas of service for God in the years ahead. Now he was facing the

*New English Bible.

stark reality that it was not to be. He felt he would never be able to preach again, that he would not live to rear his boys. He was staring into the face of death. Finally he asked for a sleeping pill. It did not put him to sleep but only caused more depression. About 1:30 A.M. he asked for another, but it too only increased the depression. He began to think that this was the way it would be the rest of his life, and it would be better to die immediately.

Early the next morning, the Reverend Richard Turnwall came to see him. Turnwall had been the previous pastor of Salem, was still a member of the church, and was now serving as director of home missions for the Minnesota Baptist Conference. Here was a man that Lindon felt he could "unload on." And he did. He expressed his pessimism: he was sure he would never be able to preach again, he would not even be able to concentrate to prepare, his ministry was finished.

Turnwall listened patiently, then grinned at him and said, "We'll see." The way he said it gave Lindon assurance that Turnwall expected him to be back. Lindon later said, "That kind of assurance drives you out of that bed, and you realize that there are people behind you, supporting you, lifting you up. Their confidence becomes your confidence."

On Wednesday I desperately wanted to spend the day with Lindon, for I felt that he needed me, but I could not because of my work. So God sent some of His other ministering angels that day. I was to learn a lot about such things in the months ahead.

Bud DeBar, moderator of the church, arrived on that Wednesday morning just as Dick Turnwall was leaving. Bud later commented, "I kept wondering what I could say to him. When I got there I realized that he did not want to be left alone, so I just stayed. I learned a lot that day. I learned that you don't need to do much talking—just listen.

He had a lot of things to wrestle through, and I just sat by. His thoughts would cycle from high to low. He had had a miserable night with an upset stomach and much pain. The French quack doctor in me kept saying, 'Maybe if you would get a little food, you'd feel better.' I guess it gave me something to say. Meanwhile, I was having my own arguments with God. At the church we had been talking about long-term plans and thinking about a possible radio ministry, since we felt that Lin would come across so well on radio. It didn't seem possible that everything could change like this.

"As I listened to him, I felt he was saying in essence, 'Why me? This can't be.' And the next minute he would be accepting it. And so the struggle waged back and forth that day. At one point he said, 'God has called me to preach and I haven't really gotten started yet.' He struggled with thoughts of his family and his concern for his boys.

"When others came to see him that day, Lin maintained an optimistic attitude. He would say honestly, 'It doesn't look good,' but he kept that hopeful note. When he was alone, he wrestled with life and death."

I quit work at noon and went to the hospital. Lin had had a very tough day, but we were able to talk and share together. Later, as I left the hospital, two doctors on the elevator asked if I were Mrs. Karo. They took time to talk with me at length, explaining the treatment they would be using. I asked them to be honest with me. Was there a good chance for Lin to be cured, or at least to have a long remission? They said they were hopeful. With the newer treatments, his chances were much better than they would have been even a year earlier. He would have five days of drugs, then sixteen days without drugs, then five more days of drugs and sixteen without. They explained that they would use two powerful drugs, Vincristine and Cytoxan, to be given in large doses, plus two drugs helpful in alleviating discomfort. He would probably be nauseated by the drugs.

I left with more hope.

I did not go to the church service that evening. Every member had been called and alerted to the seriousness of the pastor's illness. It was a hot, sticky night, but nearly 200 people assembled in the basement of the not quite completed sanctuary. Many members were out of town or on vacation, but nearly all of the adult members in town were present, plus the Lutheran pastor from the church across the street.

Moderator Bud DeBar led the meeting, but the Reverend Richard Turnwall and the Reverend Emmett Johnson were also there to help. Emmett Johnson had previously had Hodgkin's disease, and he could speak from some experience of the kind of assistance that a church can give its pastor in circumstances of great stress. Dr. Carl Christenson was also there to answer medical questions.

The congregation agreed that there must be a standby speaker for every Sunday. If Lindon felt able to speak, he would do so; if not, there would be someone else prepared. Members also felt something must be done to make it possible for me to quit work. I would learn more about that later. Most of the evening was spent in tearful prayer, with members covenanting together to pray in believing faith for his full recovery.

As they left the church, most members were experiencing what I had found even more vividly: the stunning realization that between Sunday morning when Lindon preached and this Wednesday evening, three days later, a drastic change had taken place in our plans and outlook. From now on, our lives and that of the church had to be viewed in another perspective.

3

The Battle Begins

Just for You

Dear Jesus,

I hope I'm not intruding, Lord;
This won't take too much time:
I wish to ask a favor,
For something's on my mind.

You see, I have a friend, dear Lord;
Lindon Karo is his name;
He speaks of You with words of love–
With a smile and without shame.

He's a special kind of person
With a special kind of glow–
All the makings of a great man,
Someone I'm proud to know.

He hardly even knows me,
And yet he is my friend;
For I know, if I should need him,
He's there–his hand to lend.

So, take care of pastor, Jesus;
He has so much to give!
Because of his deep faith in You,
He shows me how to live.

For I believe in pastor—
And I believe in You—
And, if faith can move a mountain,
It can make a prayer come true.
Amen

ANONYMOUS

Chemotherapy treatment began immediately on Wednesday, August 17. Lin was to have large doses of drugs for five days, then be off drugs for sixteen days; then the cycle would be repeated. The doctors told us he would probably be nauseated by the drugs. We were prepared for the worst.

But on Thursday, when I came to see him, he was a different person. The doctors had drained the fluid from his lungs, the pain was gone, he was not nauseated, and he had eaten for the first time in five days.

It seemed unbelievable and we felt that God was working a miracle. That evening, Dr. Paul Patterson, the friend who had taken us to the Vikings game the previous Saturday, came to see Lin. While he was there, another pastor came in to pray for Lin's healing. We were appreciative, for we knew that prayer was vital and that God could intervene. After he prayed, asking God to rid Lin's body of cancer, Paul leaned over and whispered to me, "He's two days too late; it has already been done!" That expression of optimism and faith was of great help to us.

On Friday, August 19, Lin was released from the hospital. We were jubilant. But the joy was dashed by the intern who released him. It was the same young man who had first told us the medical diagnosis of cancer. He said, "You shouldn't be feeling as well as you claim to feel. Maybe it is your attitude. Maybe it would be just as well to drop the drugs and just let the disease take its course."

The cruel remark was a body blow to Lin, and he felt very depressed. I was glad I still felt optimistic and could encourage him. When we got home, there was a joyful reunion between Lin and the boys. Scotty sat on his daddy's lap for a long time.

On Saturday, our house bulged with visitors. It was exhausting, but it meant a lot for Lin and me to see how the people of the church and our other friends cared so deeply.

Meanwhile, members of the church board were seeking direction from God as to what they could do. They discussed the possibility of carrying out the commandment given in James 5:14-15: "Is anyone among you sick? Let him call for the elders of the church, and let them pray over him, anointing him with oil in the name of the Lord; and the prayer of faith will restore the one who is sick, and the Lord will raise him up."

When this possibility was suggested to Lin, he immediately asked Bud DeBar, moderator of the church, to contact the board members to come on Sunday morning to have the anointing service.

It was a deeply significant hour. It was a new experience for each person who came—including Lin—and Baptist handbooks do not have a prescribed ritual for such a service. They had only those verses of Scripture to guide them. Each person placed a drop of oil on Lin's forehead, and then each person prayed for him. The love and concern they showed were in themselves a healing experience for us.

Bud DeBar later commented, "This was the first time I had ever been involved in anything like that. We got together to discuss exactly how and what we should do, what kind of oil to use, etc. At first I was fearful, but it proved to be very meaningful to me and the others."

This was the first Sunday with Lin out of the pulpit, so Bud led the worship service. He read the passage from James and told the congregation that that command had been fulfilled during the Sunday school hour.

On Sunday afternoon we gathered up a few things and left for the summer home of Floyd and Betty Dudrey, charter members of Salem Baptist. They told us we could use their cabin as long as we wanted. We thought it would be good for Lin to get away from people and really rest. I took a few days off from work.

We packed up Lin's supply of pills. The drug treatment he was on demanded that he take thirty pills a day. He had never been a pill-taker. He balked even at the suggestion of an occasional aspirin.

On Monday he took the boys fishing, but even that much exertion left him exhausted. While Lin and the boys fished, I visited with my grandmother and two great-aunts in Cambridge. They, too, were struggling with the "why" questions and they voiced them. "Why would God allow such a young, vibrant man to be cursed with this disease? Why Lin?"

I suddenly realized that I had not asked that. I would in the days to come, but up to this point God had been so very near that that particular question had not disturbed me. The question I *was* struggling with was, "What do I say to *Lin* when he is depressed with thoughts of terminal cancer?" But God gave me a sense of assurance. I don't know how to explain it, whether it was because I felt he would be healed, or just that I knew God was working in His people and in me.

On Tuesday we decided to go home. Lin was weak and somewhat depressed, and he felt it would be better to be at home.

Later in the week, when Lin felt a little better, we went out to dinner together, and for the first time he really verbalized to me his concern about the possibility of dying, and his feeling of aloneness even though he knew he was being held up by family and friends and church members.

"I feel alone, even though you care and share with me in this, and Salem is sharing. I am alone because it is *my* body that is being afflicted."

I tried to share my optimism with him; and he said, "I'm sure glad you are optimistic when I am not!"

One afternoon, Ralph Cullen called. He was a member of Salem and had been one of the visitors on that Tuesday night when the doctor announced that Lin had lymphosarcoma. Now he called and suggested that he and Lin drive over to Bethel Seminary and sit on the shores of Lake Valentine. That idea appealed to Lin, and they had a beautiful afternoon together, sitting on a hill overlooking the lake, sharing together in Scripture reading and prayer.

During the next few days there was great improvement. He regained strength and felt he would soon be able to preach again, a desire that now seemed to dominate him. And the Christian community showed love. People called, visited, wrote notes and letters of encouragement, and sent promises of constant prayer support.

And we learned that members had given sacrificially to help with our debt problem so I could quit work. We received a check for more than $4,000. Our debts were paid! Some members had given large amounts, others less. One man gave his vacation check; he decided he could stay home that summer. My last day of work was August 31. Even that was tearful. My employer and fellow employees had been so kind and understanding. On several days they had come in early to do *my* work so I would be free to visit the hospital.

The last weekend in August, my father, Lloyd Russell, came from California to see us. Lin and Dad had always hit it off well together, and in the years since our marriage they had developed a genuine father-son relationship. Lin was overjoyed at the announcement that Dad was coming.

When he arrived, I learned that he had phoned Dr. Carl Christenson before he came. He told me of the conversation. "Carl said that we can't tell how anyone's body will respond to the drugs. Lin may have three months, six months, or ten years." Dad related this to encourage me with the great possibilities available now with the drugs. It may have encouraged him, but it did not encourage me. I felt the same stab of fear I had known when the diagnosis was first made. Three months? Even ten years seemed like a short time.

I had another long talk with the Lord that night; and I was finally able to pray, "Lin is in Your hands, I know. You do all things well. Help me to remember that and to sleep well tonight with a sense of peace. Please renew the peace and optimism that I had." And I was able to sleep. The next morning I awoke with peace and optimism.

The next morning, Dad and I went to church together. It was my first time back since Lin's hospitalization, and both Dad and I had a hard time holding back the tears. The unison Scripture reading that morning was Psalm 23, and then John and Edie Holmberg sang, "He Giveth More Grace."

> He giveth more grace when the burdens grow greater;
> He sendeth more strength when the labors increase.
> To added afflictions He addeth His mercy;
> To multiplied trials, His multiplied peace.
>
> When we have exhausted our store of endurance,
> When our strength has failed ere the day is half done,
> When we reach the end of our hoarded resources,
> Our Father's full giving is only begun.
>
> Refrain:
>
> His love has no limit, His grace has no measure,
> His pow'r has no boundary known unto men;

For out of His infinite riches in Jesus,
He giveth, and giveth, and giveth again!

ANNIE JOHNSON FLINT

During that song, my heart was thumping so loudly I thought the people in the rows behind me could surely hear it. I noticed that John seemed to be having difficulty keeping his composure, so I began praying for him. That helped me, and I was able to listen and enjoy the song.

Lin seemed to gain strength with each day; and when we went down to the clinic the following Wednesday, August 30, for Lin's regular weekly tests, Dad went along.

A different intern met us, and he seemed to question whether Lin really understood what was happening to him. Lin surely did understand his medical problems, but he also understood the goodness of God in the midst of these troubles, and the goodness of the people of God. The doctor tried to explain exactly how cancer acted in the human body. Lin asked just how cancer killed a person. The doctor said that people rarely die of cancer itself, but from other illnesses, like pneumonia, that come when the body is weakened.

In the midst of this discussion, the x rays that had just been taken were returned. They showed no cancerous nodes. The tumor had disappeared! We were so jubilant that after we came home, Lin, Dad, and I played nine holes of golf. That tired Lin.

That night, Lin developed a fever that climbed to 102 degrees. By morning, the mattress was soaked in perspiration. All we could think of was pneumonia and his weakened condition. But by noon the fever was gone, and he seemed fine. That night, the fever returned. We consulted the doctor, and he said that fevers were to be expected but that Lin should rest every afternoon.

The order to rest every afternoon was not easy. Lin was an activist and a sports fan. The idea of resting during the period of the day when he felt best did not appeal to him!

My dad returned to California with a new hope in Lin's recovery.

The next Saturday, the Pattersons invited us to another Vikings football game. Lin enjoyed this one! But while sitting beside him during the game, I happened to glance at Lin's shoulder. It was covered with dark hair! The doctor had warned that he might lose his hair as a reaction to the drugs. By the time we got home, hair was coming out by handfuls, and within three days, most of his hair had fallen out. He purchased a hairpiece.

When we got home from the game, my sister and brother-in-law, Judy and Bruce Ferrin, called to ask if Lin's message the next morning would be taped. We assured them that it would, and she said that they and several of their neighbors had been praying for Lin. The neighbors had said they would like to come to the Ferrins' home and listen to Lin's first message as he faced the specter of cancer.

The next morning was Sunday, September 3, and it was Lindon's thirty-second birthday. It would be Lin's first time back in the pulpit since the fateful news. It was also Labor Day weekend, and in our suburban church there is usually an exodus on holiday weekends—especially Labor Day.

When we arrived, we found the church full! It was a great, exciting day for Lin, our family, and for Salem church. For many months he had been planning a series on the Apostles' Creed. This was the first in the series, on "I Believe in God the Father Almighty."

Although he had begun work on the series long before his onset of cancer, the message he gave that morning was deeply influenced by his new experience of facing death.

That sermon moved me and many people in the congregation. Later the tape was circulated among many friends. One of the listeners, Janelle Pearson, wrote Lin that she had opened her life to Christ as the result of hearing that sermon. Others told of gathering their neighbors together to listen to the tape, or using it in neighborhood Bible-study groups. It had an impact on many.

* * *

I Believe in God the Father Almighty

Probably all of you believe in God,
but who is the God in whom you believe?
The Greeks, in the time of Christ,
believed in many gods, and we are very critical of them.
But if we look hard at the Greeks' concept of God,
we may find that our idea of God is not too far removed.
For example, the Greeks felt
that the gods had certain things they were to do,
and that there was a kind of order in it all.
The people on earth were to match the order of the gods
and when the two were put together,
goodness and blessing would come.
Is that so different from our concept
that if we live just so, then God will bless?
We feel an inner demand for order
or life will be meaningless.

But how about the tragedies of life?
How does our understanding of God meet them?
How about that day recently when a member came and said,
"Yesterday my brother's seven-year-old daughter was
run over by a car and killed."
How does your concept of God fit into those tragedies?
Or the earthquakes and other natural disasters that
hit saints and sinners alike?

How does Vietnam fit your concept of God?
Or the fact that your pastor has cancer?

When tragedies strike, most of us tend to step back and say,
"Who is God that He permits such tragedies in life?"
If faith comes easy for you in the midst of such things,
you are different from me.

But I believe in God,
and I have found something that I think Job discovered.
I think Job had a concept of God like that of many of us,
and the devil knew how to get to him because of it.
Job figured that since God was good,
if Job lived a good life
then certainly God would reward him with good things.
It seemed to be so.

Job had a large, loving family; he had wealth.
But the devil said, "I know how to get to Job.
Take away all the good things and watch him curse God."

When Job lost all the good things and became very ill,
he was very confused.
Job did not understand at this point
what Jesus understood at the time of His death.
I find in Mark 14:32-42 what I think is the secret of
Jesus' life.
He could say, "Abba, Father."
How could Jesus face death? He believed in the father-
hood of God.

What does the "fatherhood of God" mean?
It means *mercy*.
The story of the prodigal son is the story of all of us.
We have disgraced the family of God.
We have lived for ourselves,
spent ourselves on ourselves, and reaped the consequences.

But God said, "Here I am. I love you;
I welcome you back. I'm your Father."
That's mercy.
The proof of God's mercy is seen
in the life, death, and resurrection of Jesus Christ.
What Christ did for us says,
"You are forgiven; I welcome you back."

The concept of God as Father
means not only a family relationship,
but also a relationship of authority.
When we accept Him as our Father,
we also take Him as the authority for our lives.
We are all children in this world.
Let some of the hard experiences come to us,
and we discover what children we are
and how lonely we are in this universe.
We need our Father.
Only the person who discovers God as his Father
can celebrate life despite his circumstances.

The fatherhood of God also means *intimacy.*
Romans 8:15 says that we have not been given a spirit
of fear so that we fear some kind of God up there,
but, instead, God has placed in our hearts
the spirit that cries out, "Abba, Father."
The term "Abba" is the intimate term for father
in Hebrew and Aramaic,
one of the first words an infant would learn to say.

When my two-and-one-half-year-old Scotty comes bursting
into my study,
he shouts, "Daddy!" and throws out his arms
and waits for me to pick him up.
He has something he wants to tell me.
Like little children, we have many questions about life

we do not understand; but we can come into God's presence
as we are, with all of our questions
and our stupid comments and our ignorance.
He still loves us;
He doesn't expect us to be profound
or to understand everything in life.
But we can have a relationship
of intimacy with our Father—Abba.

To believe in the fatherhood of God
also means to believe in His *goodness*.
I think we mistranslate Romans 8:28.
It should read, "God works with His people
in everything to bring about good."
That means He is working through my problems with cancer
to bring about good.
Matthew 7:9-11 says that when a little boy
comes to his father and says, "I would like some bread,"
the father doesn't pick up a rock that looks like
a bun and hand it to him saying,
"Here is your bread."
Or when a child asks for a fish,
he doesn't reach back and grab an eel
and say, "You asked for a fish; here's a kind of fish.
It's not edible, but it is a fish."
God doesn't trick us.
Romans 8:28 says that God is going to do good things for us.
When we begin to understand that God is our Father
and He does do good things,
some of our difficulties take on new meaning.

An interesting story is found in Mark 4.
The disciples are out on the Sea of Galilee, and a storm
comes up. They are about to go under when they say,
"Where's Jesus?"
Someone says, "He's sleeping at the back of the boat."

They went and grabbed Him, saying,
"What are You doing asleep?
Don't You know we are all going to die?"
Jesus said, "Oh, you of little faith."
What did He mean?
Jesus so believed in the goodness of God, His Father,
that He could sleep in the midst of the storm.

I believe the fatherhood of God was the key
to the relationship of life for Jesus,
and He gives that same relationship to us
so that we can say, as Christ did, "Abba, Father."
When Christ was going to the cross,
He said, "I don't want to go; I don't want to die."
The cross and death did not look good to Jesus.
But Christ could also say,
"Father, Your will be done."

The fatherhood of God points to our *individuality*.
There is a little game we tend to play
when we are facing death.
It's a game called "not me."
On the night the doctor told me I had cancer,
I wanted to play the "not me" game.
"John Doe could have cancer, but not me."
Another reaction comes later,
after we acknowledge the fact that we are facing death.
Then we say, "John Doe could be cured, but not me."
That's the flip side.
But a sense of the fatherhood of God came into my life
at that point, and God said,
"Wait a minute. You are not John Doe; you are Lindon Karo.
I am your Father, and I love you.
You don't know what's going to happen,
but I love you in the midst of all of this."
I stopped thinking about John Doe.

Whatever problems you are facing,
remember that God loves you.
He is your Father, and He faces those problems with you.
Do you doubt it?
Remember that Jesus suffered and died.
You can be certain that God knows what you and I are going through,
because He suffered and died, too.

The fatherhood of God also means *community.*
If God is my Father, then everyone who has Him as his Father is a part of my family.
That means we've got to be close to each other,
and we may not always get along.
I'm sure every family has some arguments,
and as in an earthly family there may be times when you'd like to trade brothers and sisters.
But we can't, for we are born into this family.
We are in it together and God is our Father.
There is something special about this family:
it is a ministering family.
When I have been too sick to feel like praying,
I knew that my family—God's people—were praying for me;
and I could relax in the love of Jesus.

The night I learned of my cancer, I was in much pain and anxiety;
I didn't sleep that night.
In the early morning hours, I said to the Lord,
"I want to go back and minister to the Salem Baptist Church,
but I guess I can't.
I'm in such pain, and it looks like this is the way it is going to be from now on."
I prayed that God would take me because I wouldn't be good for anything.
The next day Richard Turnwall came to see me,
and I told him what I had prayed

because I knew I'd not be any good as a pastor anymore.
He looked at me, smiled, and said, "We'll see."
His tone said, "We'll see how God will raise you up."
That day I got confidence from God's people—
the community of believers.
Others, young and old, have reinforced that confidence.
When I lacked it, God's people had confidence.

What does the fatherhood of God mean?
To me it means mercy,
intimacy,
goodness,
individuality,
and community.
And if you don't know God as your Father, I don't know
how you can face life—
or death.

* * *

We didn't do much to celebrate Lindon's thirty-second birthday. It was a celebration just to have him home and looking fairly good in his new hairpiece and to see him back in the pulpit with his usual vigorous style.

My brother and his family came to church that morning to hear Lindon preach, and so did my foster brother and his wife. They all came to our house for dinner. It was no fancy meal—in fact, we had tacos!

Lin also preached at the Sunday evening service. It was a very special message on a subject that was much in our thinking and in the thinking of our congregation: "Are Miracles Possible?"

Before the message, Lin did something he had been wanting to do for a long time. He told the story of David and Goliath, adapted especially for children in the audience. He told it dramatically, vigorously acting out the parts. The kids loved it, and the adults seemed to enjoy it equally.

After the evening service, there was a surprise coffee party in the church social hall in honor of Lindon's birthday. The cards he received from members and friends covered a small table. Many were humorous, some serious, but all showing love and concern. At the end of the day he was exhausted but so thankful to be back with his people.

* * *

Are Miracles Possible?

What you think of God
determines whether you really believe that miracles happen.
If you look at God
as One who stands behind this universe
and only runs the rules and laws behind this universe,
then you probably have a problem believing in miracles.
But, if you believe that God is concerned
about all His people
and that God is at work in this world,
then He must do miracles.

Now we must consider how you define a miracle.
Some of my thoughts on this subject I owe to Helmut Thielicke,
who says there are two ways to look at miracles.
He illustrates by a person
going to a place in Africa where a radio has never been
seen before. He goes into a jungle village
and turns the radio on.
The only singing these people have ever heard
is from persons whom they can see.
Now from this little box they hear a man singing.
They say, in effect, "That's a miracle."
The traveler says,
"No, no. That's not a miracle.
It merely makes use of certain laws and mechanisms.
This is no miracle."

Some people look at what God is doing or has done in the past
and say, "God only uses the laws we have in the universe
and directs things through those laws.
We are imprisoned by the natural laws of this universe.
All miracles can be described in terms of those laws."

Perhaps you define a miracle by your eyesight.
You go up into the mountains
and look at the grandeur and say,
"What a miraculous God to create these things."
And if a geologist is standing next to you,
he may say, "Oh, no. That isn't how it was done.
There were certain pressures
on the crust of the earth that brought about these mountains."
You might turn to him and say,
"I know that, but it was *God* who brought about this
great beauty and used those laws to bring it about.
He is that kind of miracle-working God."
Now, those definitions make us feel comfortable.
We do like to think God uses laws. That's how He does things.

But is that all there is in the idea of "miracle"?
Mark 2:1-12 reads,

> And when He had come back to Capernaum several days afterward, it was heard that He was at home. And many were gathered together, so that there was no longer room, even near the door; and He was speaking the word to them. And they came, bringing to Him a paralytic, carried by four men. And being unable to get to Him on account of the crowd, they removed the roof above Him; and when they had dug an opening, they let down the pallet on which the paralytic was lying. And Jesus seeing their faith said to the paralytic, "My son, your sins are forgiven." But there were some of the scribes sitting there and reasoning in their hearts, "Why does this man speak that way? He is blaspheming; who can

> forgive sins but God alone?" And immediately Jesus, perceiving in His spirit that they were reasoning that way within themselves, said to them, "Why are you reasoning about these things in your hearts? Which is easier, to say to the paralytic, 'Your sins are forgiven'; or to say, 'Arise, and take up your pallet and walk'? But in order that you may know that the Son of Man has authority on earth to forgive sins," He said to the paralytic, "I say to you, rise, take up your pallet and go home." And he rose and immediately took up the pallet and went out in the sight of all; so that they were all amazed and were glorifying God, saying, "We have never seen anything like this."

In that miracle, God clearly intervened.
That intervention went beyond the natural laws.
God did not gradually heal the man through some special medicine.
He said, "Rise up and walk."
It was a miracle.

I think there are two kinds of miracles.
I believe that God works through the courses
of events to bring about some medical breakthroughs.

When we pray for a miracle for me,
we can pray that a discovery will be made of a drug
that will eventually cure cancer.
I believe God will guide men to such knowledge,
as God's people pray.

There is another kind of miracle—the kind found in Mark 2.
Here God acted directly and instantly to bring about a miracle.
In the first kind, God is superintending the events
so that the discovery is made. In the second kind,
God just intervenes directly.

Don't misunderstand me. God is working in our midst all the time.

But there are special interventions that He sometimes makes.
I often wonder,
"Why doesn't it happen more often?"
He does intervene from time to time. But He doesn't do
it constantly.
It's like heat lightning along the path
to that goal of the fullness of the kingdom
where there will no longer be cancer,
or blindness,
or death.
And we look to that day.

Maybe God is in the process of the special intervention on
my behalf. I *feel* that He is.
And maybe on behalf of others.
And I ask, "Why not all?"
I'm not sure what that answer is,
but there is heat lightning that shows us
in the darkness of the night that He is still directing us.
There is the fullness of the kingdom yet before us
when suffering and death will be no more.
Do miracles really happen?
Yes, because that's the kind of God we have.

4

Treatments and Retreats

WE SOON BEGAN receiving cards and letters from all over the country, assuring us of prayer. People we hadn't heard from in years began corresponding. Lin was especially moved to receive letters from missionaries, assuring us that they and their friends and nationals were praying for him.

The second massive round of chemotherapy began September 6, and it made Lin too ill to preach September 10.

Each Wednesday he had to report to the St. Paul Ramsey Clinic for blood tests. At the clinic on September 13 we found many people talking about Lin's last x ray and examining it in comparison with the one showing the massive tumor. They could see no tumor. They just couldn't believe that such a large tumor could disappear in such a short time. We were much encouraged–sure that God was healing him.

On September 17, he was back in the pulpit talking about "God Almighty, Maker of Heaven and Earth." The people were eager to hear him, and this encouraged Lin. There seemed to be an electric excitement among the people, growing out of the mutual love of a pastor and his people. All seemed to feel that together we were on a great adventure of faith.

* * *

God Almighty, Maker of Heaven and Earth

What kind of a universe do we live in?
I suppose every reflective man or woman has asked
that question on some lonely night.
Do we live in a universe that is good and good for us,
or do we live in a universe of alien powers
that really is our enemy?

Our answer reveals what we think of God.
In the Apostles' Creed, one phrase deals
particularly with the subject:
I believe in God Almighty, Maker of Heaven and Earth.
If God Almighty is really the Maker of *this* heaven
and *this* earth,
and if He is *the* God Almighty and if He is a *good* God,
then that means that He is *for* us.

Some people wonder if there is a God out there at all.
They feel that their lives are controlled by fate or chance,
that life is basically meaningless.
This is a very discouraging outlook,
but there are many people who say,
"Be a realist; that's the way it is."

There are others who say, "There is a great God
behind this creation.
He set the laws in motion, but now He is separate from it."
This is known as deism.

There is another view called theism that I consider to be right.
It says that God is holy,
but He is also deeply concerned
and involved with His creation.
He has made rules for this universe,
but He is also involved in it
and in the people of that universe.

God Almighty is not only the Maker of heaven and earth,
but He is the Maker of *me*
and you.

There are two great actions of God that show Him
to be God Almighty.
The first one is recorded in Genesis 1:1,
"In the beginning *God created* the heaven and the earth."
When we read this, our twentieth-century inquisitive minds
begin asking other questions.
We want to know how He did it.
We have often asked the wrong questions about Genesis,
and when you ask the wrong questions
you come up with the wrong answers.
When I go to a math book, I do not expect to find answers
to questions of sociology or psychology.
I can only expect to find answers to math questions,
the questions it was meant to answer.
We often come to Genesis with geological questions
and biological questions
and say, "Answer this for us!"

But the writer makes it clear that he wants to talk about God.
He says: "In the beginning *God*."
The book of Revelation closes the Bible,
still talking about God.
The Bible is a *Book* about God
and about man.
The right questions to ask this Book
are the ones about the relationship of God and man.
We *can* rightfully ask, "Does God run the universe?
What are God's concerns for man?
What is man supposed to do?"
If you bring those questions to the Bible, you begin
getting answers. The first verse of the Bible sets forth
the almightiness of God,
and that He is the Creator of this heaven and this earth.

The biblical creation story says that
when God made heaven and earth He became
totally responsible for His handiwork,
and He said: "It is good."
If God made heaven and earth, then He made me;
and there will come a day when He will say:
"All right, now what did *you* do with My creation?
I lent you that body; I made you.
What have you done with it?"
To believe in God Almighty means that I must
examine my life
and choose my priorities in living.
Romans 1:20 says that man is without excuse.
We will each give an account of ourselves to the living
God. We try many ways to divert responsibility.
We may say, "It really wasn't my fault;
my mom and dad just didn't have the right genes;
that's why I am the way I am."
Romans 1:20 says we are without excuse.
We try other pleas: "You don't know my home environment;
you don't know how I grew up."
Romans 1:20 says we are without excuse.
That phrase keeps coming back. We are all accountable
before God Almighty, Maker of heaven and earth.
He is a good God, and now He says,
"What have you done with your life?"
Most people worship the creature more than the Creator,
worship self-achievement more than God.
True, God made us to achieve;
but when achievement takes top priority in our lives,
we are worshiping ourselves rather than God.
So we must ask, "Where does God fit into our lives?"
Where does God fit into your occupation?
Where does God fit into your family?
Where does God fit into the development of your children?
Where does God fit into your relationship
with the people at work?

There is another way that God acts in our lives.
I experience the almightiness of God through *His new creation.*
Genesis 1:2 says that the earth originally
was a place of chaos—void,
a world without form or meaning.
God moved upon it and gave it form and meaning.

But how about the chaos of life—your personal chaos,
the chaos of this world,
the perversion of good in my life and the world,
the exploitation of creation?
Does God have a remedy for this kind of chaos?

None of us can easily forget Munich,
nor the Middle East; we cannot forget Vietnam,
or the racial problems that we have here in the United States.
And none of us can easily forget
the internal chaos we experience—
the selfishness, greed, and lust
that roam inside of us.
Where is power to change us?
Where does God Almighty come into my life?
How does the Maker of Lindon Karo
make him a loving person,
delivering him from the power of selfish existence?

Paul says that he is not ashamed of the Gospel
because *it* is the power [the "almightiness"] of God
to bring about salvation to everyone who has faith
(Romans 1:16).
It is the action of God in Jesus Christ
that makes power available for every human being.
We need no longer live entrapped by our self-centered lives.
We now can have a new kind of life,
a new sufficiency in our relationship to God.

The coming of Christ into the world was itself an act of power.
It appeared to be an act of weakness.
Here was a small child growing up in an obscure
Galilean village. When He became a young man,
His teaching opposed much of the teaching of His day.
But the combination of what He taught
and what He did was making a very important announcement:
"My coming is not that of just another human being coming
into this world, but it is a great release of power."
He said, "If I cast out demons by the finger of God,
then the kingdom of God has come upon you" (Luke 11:20).
When Christ came,
the forces of evil were dealt their final deathblow
and the possibility of a new way of life
was opened to all mankind.
The almightiness of God became available through
what Christ did for us.

There are two important words that Paul uses in Romans 1:16,
words intimately related to the almightiness of God.
The first word is *salvation,*
a rich word with profound meanings.
First, it means *help.*
Men have always had many physical, emotional, and
spiritual needs.
When Christ came, He said that salvation
had come for mankind.
It meant His hearers were going to experience
help for their bodies and help for their souls.

Salvation also means *freedom.*
The word suggests that man is entrapped
in a certain kind of life,
but new power is now open to him.

He is free to live in relationship to God,
released from enslavement to greed and lust.
He is *free* to enjoy God, to love God's creation,
to live the kind of life God intended for him.

Salvation means *discovery*.
Man is traveling down the wrong road, lost
in his own self-centered sin, and God finds him
and puts him on a road that has meaning
and relationship with Him and a goal.
Discovery is a part of salvation.

Salvation means *pardon*.
The wrath of God is mentioned in Romans 1.
There is judgment for sin.
There is judgment in this life,
and there is judgment at the final time.
But salvation means we are pardoned.
There are certain things that I do right,
but there are also things I am ashamed of.
But God says, "In salvation you are pardoned."
Suddenly this person who is guilt-ridden
experiences new freedom
and a sense that he is pardoned by God.

Salvation means *hope*.
This implies that salvation is not fully experienced here.
God doesn't end it all here in this world.
Death is not the end.
There is a new world that God is going to bring about.

Salvation gives us *security*.
God says, "Come into My family."
You feel secure in the family of God.
The almightiness of God brought salvation
that gives us all these things.
But they are contingent on the second word, *faith*.

Faith really grows by stages. A man must first be receptive.
He must want to find out about God.
Mental assent is often the second step.
You may give mental assent
to what you are reading by thinking,
"Yes, I agree those things are true."
This is an important step, but it is not faith.
Faith comes when we *act* on what we assent to.
We must say, "Yes, it is true and I surrender myself
to those truths and I make them my way of life.
God is my God;
Christ is my Saviour;
He is the Lord of my life,
and now I'm going to live in that direction."
That is the step of faith.
Now you have gone from allegiance to self
to allegiance to God.
You have discovered the lordship of Christ,
and God has become to you
the Almighty, Maker of heaven and earth.

Even when we are experiencing the graces of God's salvation,
we face situations and problems
in which we do not seem to know the almightiness of God.
What then?
Jesus says in Matthew 10:29,
"Are not two sparrows sold for a cent?"
Sparrows may not be worth anything to men,
and yet when a sparrow falls to the ground, God knows it.
God knows and cares about the significant
and the insignificant things in our lives.
He knows every tough problem we face.
Second Corinthians 9:8 adds another idea:

> And it is God's power to provide you richly with every good gift. Thus you will have ample means in yourselves to meet

> each and every situation with enough and to spare for every good cause (NEB*).

God gives grace and He gives His presence;
  He gives strength for every situation you will ever face,
    and He gives it in such abundance
  that you will have enough left over to give to others.
    That's the kind of God we have.

Do we live in a friendly universe with a good God?
  Yes! He is the Maker of heaven and earth.
    He is the Maker of *me*.
      He shared my human plight
  and knows the temptations of humanity.
    Therefore I know He cares.
  Every action of God spells almighty concern for me.

* * *

Clinic tests on September 20 were good again, and there was a new surge of encouragement. He was working hard on his sermon for September 24: "I Believe in Jesus Christ, His Only Son, Our Lord."

But on that Sunday morning, Lin woke me at 4 A.M. He had severe pain in the left side of his chest, very similar to the pain he had experienced at Trout Lake Camp. The pain did not subside, so at 4:30 I called Dr. Luigi Taddeini, who was the specialist in charge of Lin's case. He told me to bring Lin down immediately. He checked in at about 5 A.M. I was frightened, and Lin was frightened. I prayed a lot, and among other things, I asked God for others to pray with me so I would not be praying alone. Later, two women from the church, Edie Holmberg and Beverly Kinsman, recounted that they had awakened very early that same morning with a great burden to pray for Lin.

At 6:30 I realized some provision had to be made for the morning service, so I called Berkeley Mickelsen, a professor

*New English Bible

at Bethel Seminary and a member of Salem, told him the situation, and asked him to take over for Lin. He accepted gladly.

And then, almost as quickly as it had come, the pain was relieved with the help of codeine. The blood tests and x rays had been negative, and the doctor said Lin could go home and preach if he wanted to. He *did* want to. I called Berkeley back and he said, "Are you sure he feels well enough? He is too valuable to us. He was one of the best students I ever had and among those with the highest potential and ability."

When I repeated that conversation to Lin, it did wonders for his morale.

Lin did preach that morning, on "I Believe in Jesus Christ, His Only Son, Our Lord."

* * *

Jesus Christ, His Only Son, Our Lord

Who really is Jesus Christ?
  This question has haunted people of inquisitive minds
  through the ages since His death and resurrection.
    When we read about His life,
  we can't help seeing that Jesus is different.
    He didn't fit the mold of the religious leaders
  or political leaders of His day.

    He doesn't fit the mold for our day, either.
    Look at the men He drew around Him.
  They were neither popular nor intellectual.
  By our standards, they were a group of losers.
  Until after Jesus' death and resurrection,
  none of them made any mark even in their own small land.
    Jesus seemed to make a lot of political blunders.
  He lunched with men like Zacchaeus,

who was looked down upon by most people.
He made friends with the woman at the well,
who was socially rejected in that community.
Even worse, He was not tactful to the religious leaders
of that day.
His teachings cut across their ideas,
and He didn't seem to care how they reacted.

Jesus did a lot of things that looked like blunders
if He really wanted to bring about some change in His world.
Yet, every honest student of history must admit
that no man ever changed history as Jesus Christ did.
We even date our calenders from the year of His birth.
Every person who writes a date
is saying that when Jesus Christ came to this earth,
He became the focal point of history.
He has already made a profound effect on your life,
even if you are not one of His followers.

What should be our attitude toward Jesus Christ,
and how do we really get to know Him?
There has been, for the last two centuries,
a movement called "The Search for the Historical Jesus."
Some scholars feel that the biblical accounts
are encrusted with stories that seek to enhance Jesus,
but are really fabrications of the culture of that time.
They say we must somehow get behind the stories
and find the real Jesus.
So they try to "peel back" the stories.
But they have found that peeling back the stories
is like peeling back an onion.
No matter how far down you peel, you still have an onion.
No matter how you look at the Gospel records,
Christ still comes through as a Transformer of lives.

Some people wish that the Gospel writers
had been more objective, that they had given

only straight facts as impartial observers.
But no man was ever an impartial observer
of Jesus Christ. Jesus Christ made claims
upon the lives of the persons He encountered,
and men had to respond either for Him or against Him.

Each of the four gospel writers—Matthew, Mark, Luke, and
John—either had experiences with Jesus Christ
or drew his material from those who did have
firsthand experiences with Christ.

It is difficult for us to discuss with total objectivity
any *experience* we have had.
We each see it against our own background of feelings,
previous experiences, etc.
If five witnesses observed the same automobile accident,
each would see it differently
and react to it differently.
And the five stories would give a more complete picture,
even though there may be some minor discrepancies,
than you would get from one account
of an "objective" observer.

We should learn from this
not to stereotype anyone's experience with Christ.
Each of us who is committed to Christ
has had a unique experience in that encounter.
No two are identical.

In our desire to know Jesus Christ,
the Bible has given us some important helps.
Among these helps are the names ascribed to Jesus.
These names help us experience more of Christ.

The first title is the "Son of Man."
Our first impulse is to assume

that means Christ was totally human like me.
But as soon as I say that, I draw back
because there are monsters of
greed, lust, hate, and resentment in my life.
We have no evidence
that Jesus had those monsters within Him.
The truth is that Christ was
the *only* "totally human" Person this world
has ever seen.
He is the one who demonstrates what man is supposed to be.
Some of us know we are far from what we should be,
but there is some standard inside us,
pointing to what we ought to be.

We observe the life of Christ
and we see man as God intended.
Some people are troubled
about Jesus' obvious reliance upon the Father,
but that's what man is intended to be.
Note the attitude that Jesus had toward people,
His compassion and concern.
There were blind persons whom other people tripped over;
there were crippled persons whom other people kicked,
but Jesus treated them as persons of worth.
We don't reach that standard.
Yet Jesus was human, of the same flesh,
the same drives as we know.
We cannot use the excuse, "Oh, but I'm just a human being,
and human beings err; therefore, I am really not accountable."
Jesus Christ says, in effect,
"Here's the life."

The contrast could plunge us into despair.
That is what happened to the prodigal son
when he thought about his home
and what his father was like.

He said, "I am not fit to be my father's son."
When we look at Jesus Christ, the Son of Man,
and see how far we miss the mark,
we can fall before God and say,
"I am not fit to be called Your son;
I am not fit to be in Your family."

The title Son of Man also means that
He has so identified with me that He knows what I face.
When I face death,
I know He struggled with it.
When I feel lonely,
I know He felt lonely.
When I feel misunderstood,
I know He has had the same feeling.
He knows what it is to be human and to live in frustrations.

But Jesus is more than the Son of man;
He is the Son of God.
Now, "Son of man" means He is manlike,
and "Son of God" means He is Godlike.
I do not really understand how the two can be put together.
There are many people who do things that are Godlike,
but that doesn't mean they are *the* sons of God.
Christ is the *only* Son of God.
He has a unique relationship with the Father.
This is confessedly difficult ground,
involving what we call the Trinity.

Jesus Christ also is called God.
Therefore, we may think, "Why call Him the Son of God?
Why not just call Him God?"
The doctrine of the Trinity says
that God the Father is a person;
God the Son is a person;
God the Holy Spirit is a person.

Three persons but one God.
It is a paradox.
But we are talking about God, not a human being.
We as human beings
are left at the mercy of His revelation,
and His revelation says that God is the Father,
God is Jesus Christ,
and God is the Holy Spirit.
John 3:16 says that Jesus is the only begotten Son of God.
We humans beget offspring who are equally human with us.
God the Father begat His Son who was equally God with Him.
When I read about Jesus and His life,
I am reading about God.
If I have a question about the love,
concern, and compassion of God,
I read about Jesus
and I can see the love and concern that God has toward me.
Christ did not simply talk about God,
but He said that those who saw Him were seeing God.

The coming of God into the world in Christ
is the most significant event in history.
It is the greatest miracle the world has ever known.
If you think Jesus Christ is counterfeit,
that He is not actually God,
then you might as well forget Him.
All of His promises are worthless.
He said that you can be forgiven
by committing your life to Him,
that He has paid the price for you,
that you can be made right with God,
that God will accept you, and that God loves you.

But if Jesus Christ was counterfeit,
then you can't believe any of that.

If He is not who He said He was,
how can you trust what He said?
He is either the Son of God,
the revelation of God, or He is not!

There is a third title given to Christ
which follows the first two naturally.
This title is "Christ, the Lord."
The title "Son of God" shows Christ's relationship to God the Father. The title "Christ the Lord" defines my personal responsibility to Him.

First Corinthians 6:19-20 says,

> Do you not know that your body is a temple of the Holy Spirit who is in you, whom you have from God, and that you are not your own? For you have been bought with a price: therefore glorify God in your body.

When Paul wrote this, he was using an illustration
from the cultural practice of his time known as manumission.
Slavery was common in New Testament times.
Many slaves longed to be free.
There was only one sure way you could gain freedom
if you were a slave and that was to buy it.
Slaves were often paid a few pennies a day.
Some of them took every penny they earned
and deposited it in the temple of a god of their choice.
When they had the amount prescribed–
it might take half a lifetime –
they could purchase themselves from their master.
At that time, the slave and his master
would go to the temple, take the money and say in essence,
"I am taking the money from this god
and giving it to you. That god is buying me;
here is the price."
Paul used that illustration to say that God, in effect,
bought us and now we are to serve Him, not ourselves.

He is the Lord Jesus Christ.
Jesus was a common name in the first century.
One historian records twenty men by the name of Jesus.
There were five high priests in Jewish history
with the name Jesus.
That tells us something about His identity.
He took a common name, Jesus.
But "the Christ" means more.
It means the anointed One, the Messiah,
the long-awaited One, the revelation of God,
the One who is said to be God with us.
He is the human Jesus,
but He is also the Christ who is divine, the Son of God.
He is Lord, the Master of your life.
He bought you; He has paid the price!
The title "Lord Jesus Christ" says it all.

Another title used of Him is Saviour, or Mediator.
All of us need a Saviour, a Mediator,
because we are sinners.
We need Someone who will make our lives right with God.
Perhaps our situation is like that of a car
and its speedometer on which every mile is recorded.
As we go through life, our actions are registered every day.
At the end of that registration
is an entry common to all men: "Death Sentence."

This is not a popular idea in our day.
We like to think that everyone somehow makes it.
The Scriptures say otherwise.
However, there is a provision recorded in Colossians 2:13-14:

> And you . . . God made alive together with him, . . . having canceled the bond which stood against us with its legal demands; this he set aside, nailing it to the cross (RSV*).

*Revised Standard Version.

What we have done has sentenced us.
But God says there is a higher power
in the action of Jesus Christ for us,
and that higher power
has erased that damning registration
and now can make all men right with God.

Last Thursday night I had a startling experience.
I went to bed about ten o'clock,
and all of a sudden I heard a news item on the television
in the living room to the effect
that we may have a breakthrough in cancer treatment.
I jumped out of bed, ran into the living room,
and listened carefully.
It wasn't quite as promising as I had hoped,
but I thought, *What an idiot I would be,*
if there were found a cure for cancer,
but I just foolishly or ignorantly went on
in a cancerous condition and died.
It is equally ridiculous for us to go on
in our sinful state when God says:
"I will be your God; I want you to know life."

Jesus Christ is God's Son, our Lord,
and He has provided the way.

* * *

On Tuesday, September 28, Lin was scheduled to go as guest speaker to the Bethel Seminary retreat for new and returning students. The date had been made long before Lindon found he had cancer, and now he was thrilled to find that he felt well enough to keep this commitment.

He rode to the camp with Emmett Johnson, executive director of the Minnesota Baptist Conference. He was to talk about the ministry of preaching, a subject dear to him. He said little about his illness at the retreat, but the news of it had spread rapidly among the students and they hung on his words. He talked about his view of the ministry and of the Church. He told them that the pastor must be a priest, ministering to people on behalf of God. His excitement with the work of proclaiming God's Word was contagious among the students.

Because of beginning another round of chemotherapy, Lin did not preach on October 1.

On October 2 and 3, we were invited to participate in the Shalom Conference of Minnesota Baptist Conference pastors and their wives. It is a time to share what God has been doing in lives, to share hurts, to encourage one another, to pray and share around God's Word.

During the course of the two-day conference, we met in small groups, and Lin was able to share what he called his adventure with dying. For the first time I saw Lin cry in public, but the experience was good for him and for me. It was helping him to lower the guard that he had used since childhood to protect him from emotional hurts. Perhaps his best experience came with another pastor when the two of them were able to share freely—and with tears—their deep feelings about situations each was facing.

5

Return to Normalcy

LIN CONTINUED to have some very good days, so good that he was even able to play tennis, handball, and golf, all of which he enjoyed immensely.

He was also able to enjoy his usual activities with the boys. Rob especially liked to wrestle with his dad. Each night, after supper, Rob would say, "Can we wrestle tonight, Dad?" And Lin would get down on his knees on the floor and the kids would come running at him, trying to get him down. As hard as they tried, Lin always came out victor. Rob would tell him how unfair it was. "Don't use both hands this time, Dad." And away they would go again, loving every minute of it, win or lose.

Sunday, October 8, was another good day, and Lin preached on "Who Was Conceived by the Holy Ghost, Born of the Virgin Mary."

* * *

Who Was Conceived by the Holy Ghost Born of the Virgin Mary

We often approach the virgin birth of Christ
feeling that we have to prove it.
And in trying to do that,

we may miss some of what God was telling
His people through this event.

In Genesis 3:15 we have an account
of God talking to Satan.
He said something was going to happen between
Eve and Satan. From Eve's seed,
Satan was to be bruised. It would be a deathblow,
even though Satan would be able to strike back.
Satan would be limited in his power,
and from Eve's seed would come a great victory.
All the events of the Old Testament were
only precursors of *the* event of history,
the birth of Jesus Christ.

Now try to picture with me that scene recounted in Luke.
Here is Mary, betrothed to Joseph.
The biblical betrothal was a much firmer relationship
than our kind of engagement.
They were in all essence married,
except that they did not have sexual relations.
However, the relationship was so close
and so important
that it was looked upon as binding.
It usually lasted about one year.
If Joseph had died during this time,
Mary would have been considered a widow.

During this betrothal period, an angel told Mary she was going
to have a baby. Imagine her confusion.
"How can I have a baby? I have had no relations with a man.
How is that possible?"
The angel said it was to be a unique birth,
made possible by the miraculous work of the Holy Spirit.
As a further sign,
her fellow kinswoman, Elizabeth,
in her old age, also was to give birth.

And as a sign that this was of God,
Mary was to go to Elizabeth and verify what was happening to her.

Then came trauma: How would she tell Joseph?
How could she tell such a thing to this good man whom she loved?
Mary probably was only fourteen or fifteen.
It must have been an extremely traumatic experience for her.
But out of this event,
we get a clue as to how God comes into life.
He doesn't, like Zeus, touch down on Mount Olympus and wave, "Hi, humanity."
Instead, God comes to us in the form of a baby,
entrusts Himself to the care of a young girl,
entrusts Himself to the relationship that Mary and Joseph have.

It was a world vexed with human problems.
Authorities of that day were trying to find out
what the population was so that the people could be taxed.
Mary and Joseph were ordered to go to the city
of their family, Bethlehem. Bethlehem was overcrowded.
Of course, the innkeeper was concerned
about getting whatever he could from the people,
and his place was packed out.
How could he worry about a woman
who was about to give birth?
Unannounced and almost incognito,
God's Son came into this world through Mary.
In the midst of the world and its human needs, the Son of God was born to a young couple.

How does God come into your life?
He physically came into this world
through an ordinary and an extraordinary birth,
but how does He come into your life?

He comes to us through human experiences
and daily problems that we face.
God in Christ came into our world
and struggled along with us.
He knows our problems.
He desires to share His life with you.

Jesus was born in a crowded barn with all of the stench
that went with it.
The innkeeper had no time to deal with the problem.
Perhaps that is symbolic of the way we treat God
most of the time.
The world couldn't afford to take time for the problems
of Christ, the God-man,
and we, too, seem too busy to give Him time.

This is basically a matter of our life-style.
What part does God have in your life-style?
Are we forcing Him out
because we make other things so important?

The birth of Jesus shows that Jesus is not only God but also a
part of humanity.
He is part of us.
He is wedded to my life and will struggle with me.
He knows from experience how people respond to me—
sometimes with anger, hatred, resentment,
and sometimes with love, joy, and compassion.
He has felt the hatred and the jealousy of men.
When we come to God with our problems,
we can say, "Here I am,
a human being in a world with problems,
and, God, I am having a tough time."
He knows from experience how hard it is.

If God had not visited us the way He did in Christ,
we really could not be sure

that He knows the problems we face.
Jesus Christ, our Saviour, was born into this world,
entrusted to Joseph and Mary.
In manhood He was recognized by some as the Son of God.
He was crucified, dead, and buried.
But He rose from the dead.
Since Christ shared all the ills of mankind,
we know that as God's people
we cannot expect some preferential treatment.
But whatever we face, He has already faced.
When I have my bad days,
when I know the disease and discouragement I am facing,
how do I know God really cares?
I look at Jesus Christ and His life.
He did not cop out.

There is an interesting article in *Eternity* magazine
by Joe Bayly about King Hezekiah.
King Hezekiah was about to die,
and he said, "Lord, I don't want to die."
He wept.
And the Lord gave him fifteen more years.
But then Isaiah came to him and said,
"King Hezekiah, I have a message from the Lord.
This nation is going to be overrun.
It is not going to happen under your rule and reign,
but it is going to happen in the future
and your sons will be taken into captivity."
And Hezekiah said, "Whoopie!
It's not going to happen in my reign."
Hezekiah really copped out.

Do we sometimes think,
"If it is not going to happen to me,
why should I be concerned?"
Sometimes we may think, "Perhaps the Lord will come back
shortly and it won't be my problem."

Even that may be a cop-out.

If God is wedded to human life,
then I, too, must be wedded to this life
with its human problems,
and I cannot excuse myself by saying,
"Someday I am going to escape from these problems."
Instead, I take Christ into this human life
and I struggle with my problems
and those of the society in which I live.
I say, "Yes, since those are God's problems,
they are also my problems."
Since God is wedded to human life, all who follow Him
are likewise wedded to human life and its problems.
As God's people, we are to do what we can
to correct those problems.
Sometimes a religious experience can so lift us out of
human problems that we feel we don't have to face them.
But an experience with God
should not become an escape from the realities of life.
As we become closer to God,
we should become more sensitive to human problems.
The story of the birth of Christ shouts that to me.
God came to the one-horse town of Bethlehem,
so crowded that He had to be born in a barn,
and very few realized the significance of the happening.

The virgin birth teaches me that Jesus Christ is from among us, as man,
and that He is also from above us, as God.
We usually express this by saying that Jesus is human
and also divine.
The Bible says He was conceived by the Holy Spirit.
Did the life of Jesus Christ validate that claim?

Consider this incident from Luke 5.

Peter and his partners had been fishing all night
and they had caught nothing.
Jesus saw them and He said, "I will tell you where to fish."
The men did not know Him and may have thought,
"Who does this guy think he is
that he can tell us where to fish?"
But they gave it a try, and they made a big catch.
If somebody told you a good place to fish
and you went and caught some,
your reaction would be to say,
"Hey, thanks a lot, buddy. That's a great fishing hole."
That was not Peter's reaction.
Instead, Peter fell down before Jesus and said,
"Depart from me, I am a sinful man."
He suddenly realized that Jesus
was more than just a man.

If you'll start reading about Jesus Christ with an open mind,
you may make the same discovery.
Consider those who followed Jesus.
They all started with a human Jesus.
He told people to follow Him
because He knew that as they followed Him
and as He taught them, they would be drawn unto Him.
And if you are struggling with believing in Jesus,
start reading about His life.
Like the disciples, you may discover that there is more
to this Jesus than just a human man.

With the Holy Spirit using the human life of Christ,
you may be drawn into the second great teaching—
that Jesus is not only from among us,
but also from above us. He is not only man; He is God.
You may find yourself falling on your knees and saying,
"My Lord and God."

When the Bible says that Jesus was conceived
by the Holy Spirit, it is saying that He is from above.
Ultimately all our human problems end in frustrations.
But if Jesus is from above, that is, if He is God,
and He comes into the midst of those problems,
He brings meaning to life.
Death, the great enemy of us all, is not the end.
Jesus Christ is concerned about us.
And if we live in relationship to Him,
we discover meaning and purpose in life.

So the virgin birth is not an idea about which to argue.
Instead, it shows us the two basic truths:
that Jesus is from us, a man,
and Jesus is from above, God.
Christ was usual human flesh in that He was a man;
but He was also God, so He was
unusual in the living out of that human life.

Jesus Christ never expected those who followed Him
to understand and accept all of this from the beginning.
We only learn and experience these truths
by walking through life with Him.
I find Him wedded to my human life;
I find Him coming into my problems
and giving me power to deal with them.

Helmut Thielicke said that in his first experience
with abstract art, he had no appreciation for it at all.
Then one day someone gave him a book about some of the
impressionistic artists, and he started reading about
their lives and their art.
Then he found himself drawn to their art.
The profound teachings about Jesus Christ
and the Christian life carry no meaning to us
until we meet the Artist of life,
Christ Himself.

When we meet Him, these truths come alive
with significance and meaning.

I believe in Jesus Christ,
conceived of the Holy Ghost,
born of the virgin Mary.
God Himself has come to share our lives and empower us.

* * *

The following week Lin's mother and stepfather, Irma and Ralph Smith, came from California for a week's visit. It was a week of good fellowship. One evening we were able to go down to Minneapolis to eat in an Italian restaurant, even climb the stairs to the second floor, and enjoy our meal and our time together. Lin loved Italian food, so this was a special treat.

The four of us were able to watch Steve play in two of his Little League football games on cold, cold days, although our California parents didn't come dressed for such weather. Lin kept warm by running up and down the sidelines while Steve made a couple of touchdowns and several good plays for additional yardage.

Lin's folks were in church to hear Lin preach on October 15 on a difficult subject, "Suffered Under Pontius Pilate." It was the last time they would hear him preach.

* * *

Suffered Under Pontius Pilate

There is one question most of us probably want to ask God
when we see Him.
"God, why, when You have so much power,
do people have to suffer?
Why is there so much pain in this world?"

We know that some kinds of pain are essential for health.

When you put your hand on a hot stove,
pain tells you to jump back.
Otherwise you would just start burning.
But there are other kinds of suffering
in which no good is apparent.
It is difficult for me to see meaning
in the kinds of suffering that I experience with cancer.
I thank God for what He has done so far,
but I sometimes find myself asking,
"Why, God?"

We ask why there is suffering and pain,
and we find that Christ came to us
as a man with the capacity to suffer like us.
Suffering is a part of life
and our God chose to suffer with us
when He took on Himself human flesh.
It is through the suffering of Christ
that we begin to understand God
and His care for us.

Christ on the cross endured extreme physical suffering.
But there is also another kind of suffering that
Christ endured which is akin to much of our suffering.
Most of us have suffered loneliness.
Most of us know what it is to be misunderstood, rejected.
Christ went through that same kind of human suffering.
He was sent to bring mankind back to God.
He reached out, bringing God's message to men,
but there was little response. He was ignored.
Men talked about God;
they said they were concerned about God,
but they ignored the real God among them.

Christ was a man who enjoyed every sunrise
and every sunset
and every springtime and every harvest.

He loved children and their laughter.
You know from your own experiences that if something
is gnawing at you, it somehow clouds your whole life.
Christ in the springtime, in the sunshine,
with the laughing children,
could not enjoy life as He wanted because He knew
this haunting truth:
man was not right with God.
See Christ as He looked over Jerusalem.
"I would love to have gathered you together like a hen
does her little chickens, but *you would not!*"
There was a continual longing in Jesus' life:
"I would like to have brought you back to God.
I would like to have helped you come to know my Father,
but *you would not.*"
That kind of suffering overshadowed all of Christ's life.

Christ also suffered rejection.
Christ knew that some people would reject Him.
We all know there are some people who will not like us.
That is just part of the way we and others are put together.
In Christ's life He knew He was going to run counter
to some religious leaders.
They were going to reject Him.
He could chalk them off.
He knew there were others who were out for their own
selfish ends and they would not like His teachings.
He could chalk them off.
What hurt Him most was that crucial night all alone
with those closest to Him,
His disciples,
who could not stay awake to support Him in prayer
when He *needed* them,
and was facing His most critical hour.

Do you know what times I dread the most?

I hate the nights full of pain.
Perhaps some of you know what it is like
to suffer—
alone—
at night.
Christ experienced that.
He knew that men would soon be coming out to arrest Him,
that He would go on trial and be rejected.
On that lonely dark night
He didn't have even His disciples to encourage Him.

When Jesus was on the cross there was a small group
of loved ones gathered there.
That must have been some encouragement for Him.
But they were gathered to weep for the physical pain
He was suffering. Their Friend was dying.
They weren't gathered to say to the world,
"Listen, Jesus *is* the Son of God.
We weep for our own sin and the sin of mankind
that would do this to the Son of God."
Christ knew that even at the end there were few, if any,
who really grasped what He was doing.
Most of us know that misunderstanding brings
great suffering.

Christ not only understood humanity,
but He understands my suffering when I am misunderstood.
Christ tells me by His suffering
that His love was so great that He entered
suffering for us.

Christ suffered apathy,
He suffered rejection,
and Christ also suffered injustice.
Pilate must have been a good officer in the army and
a good administrator or he would not have been given
the responsibility of governing Judea.

The account of Christ's trial shows that Pilate said,
"I find nothing wrong with this man.
I cannot have Him crucified. You take Him!"

When we read the account of the trial we say,
"Did Pilate really try?"
Pilate really did try to help Jesus.
He tried to get Him off
by reminding the Jews of their custom to have a prisoner
released at Passover time. He thought they would say,
"Fine, Jesus can be released."
Instead they said, "No, give us the insurrectionist;
give us Barabbas."
We may ask why Pilate didn't simply say to them,
"Listen, he is an innocent man, and I as the governor
of this country cannot have him sentenced to death."
Why didn't he say that? Life is very complicated.
Pilate had struck out three times with the Jewish people.
Pilate had moved the army headquarters from
Caesarea to Jerusalem.
In doing this, he brought the standards
that bore the image of the emperor, Tiberius, to Jerusalem.
Caesar was a god to the Roman government.
Therefore, when Pilate marched into Jerusalem with
the standards, the Jewish people objected vehemently
because they felt it was causing them to worship graven
images.
A delegation was sent to Pilate to discuss the problem,
but Pilate said, "I won't hear of any of this.
If anyone tries to stop me, I'll just kill him."
And the people lay down before him and said,
"Kill us. We'll die for it."
That would cause too much trouble for Pilate
as a new ruler in Judea.
So he gave in and took the standards down.

Pilate's second failure came when he decided

he would place a series of shields in his palace.
The shields bore the names of the Roman gods.
In the people's eyes,
they also constituted graven images.
This time the people took their grievances to Tiberius,
the emperor, and said they wanted the shields taken down.
The emperor came back to Pilate and said, "Take them down."
Pilate had two strikes against him.

Pilate's third failure came by way of a very neat plan.
Jerusalem needed more water
and Pilate came up with a plan to get more water
into Jerusalem. But he didn't have the money to finance
the project so he decided to take it out
of the Temple treasury.
But to the Jews that money was holy,
reserved for God.
The people rebelled against Pilate.
Pilate ordered his troops to restore order.
However, his soldiers got out of hand,
and many people were massacred.
And now these same people say to Pilate
at the trial of Jesus,
"If you release this man,
you are not Caesar's friend;
everyone who makes himself a king
sets himself against Caesar."
It was a tough situation.
The Jews were saying,
"If you decide not to crucify Jesus Christ,
we will report you to Caesar
and you know what he will do to you.
So either you keep your job and crucify Christ,
or you release Him and lose your job."
Pilate had to choose between truth (principle)
or his career. Life is often like that.

We look at Pilate and say, "Pilate tried."
I think every human being tries.
But when a man places his own interests
above what is right, he causes suffering.
In Pilate's case, it was Christ who suffered.

How do you respond to life's complicated situations?
Are you suffering from the injustices of others,
or are you causing others to suffer
by your own acts of injustice?
Christ's suffering was for us.
How do I know that God cares for me?
Because Christ suffered.

If you do not believe in Jesus Christ
as your Lord and Saviour,
I do not know what you do in the midst of *your* suffering.
But Christ means a great deal to me
in the midst of my suffering.
Because I know He, too, suffered,
He knows what I need.
And if He made it with His suffering,
I can make it with mine.
Can you make it with yours without Him?

6

Growing Pain and Growing Fellowship

THE FOLLOWING DAY, October 16, after his parents left, Lin began to feel quite ill, with headaches and much pain. By Tuesday, the right side of his face was beginning to feel numb and his fingers tingled. On Wednesday evening, he called to me in distress, "Come quickly." He was seeing everything double. We immediately called Dr. Taddeini. He told Lin to come to the hospital the next morning. He sounded concerned.

I was frightened. And because Lin seemed alarmed, our boys were frightened. They had never seen their dad upset like this before. Steve could not go to sleep, so we talked awhile and finally Lin got up and went to his bedroom; that simple act reassured Steve.

That night as I lay in bed, I knew again the cold fingers of fear around my heart. But as I faced the uncertain future, there was a peace that God would give me grace for whatever lay ahead.

On Thursday morning, we went to the hospital, thinking his vision would be checked in the out-patient clinic. We found orders that he was to be admitted to the hospital. The doctors wanted to find whether his new pain and double vision were due to drug reaction, a virus, or another tumor developing somewhere. Tests for the next few days were inconclusive, and he was given a black patch for his left eye so that it would not be used. A neurologist came in to explain that his eye damage *could* be permanent. That was discouraging! Later, Dr. Taddeini said he did not think it would be permanent; they were taking him off the drugs he was then on, and eventually the nerves would heal and his sight return to normal.

They gave no clues as to when Lin would be released. That should have warned me that the cancer was returning, but I was too optimistic to recognize it.

On October 26, when Lin had been back in the hospital for a week, Dr. Carl Christenson and Gordy Lindquist were visiting one evening and suggested that I go with them for coffee and a piece of pie. That night Carl told me that Lin's situation was deteriorating. The drugs were not doing what they were expected to do. His condition was now called lymphosarcoma leukemia in the acute stage. "Lin has about a fifty-fifty chance," Carl said. I maintained my composure until I reached home. Then I cried until I felt there were no tears left. I called my parents and a few close friends, and we wept across the lines.

That night I felt absolutely helpless. What did the future hold? How long did Lin have? What could I tell Steve and Rob? "Help, God! Help!" was all I could say.

Later I read Isaiah 43:2-3: "When you pass through deep waters, I am with you, when you pass through rivers, they will not sweep you away; walk through fire and you will not be scorched, through flames and they will not burn you. For I am the LORD your God, the Holy One of Israel, your deliverer" (NEB).

The waters and the flames were there, but so was God.

The next morning, I had to go to the hospital and, for the first time in our married life, hide something from my husband. When visitors came, I would go down to the cafeteria with them and cry; then I would go back up to the seventh floor and attempt to act normal.

Later in the afternoon, I came back to his room to see two doctors talking with Lin. As I entered, Lin said, "Things don't look so good."

And I only said, "I know." It was such a relief to have Lin know so that we could share together our disappointment and questions about life and death and pain. And share we did. That was one of the first times I heard him say, "When I go, I want to go in a blaze of glory."

Lin had been told that Kathryn Kuhlman would be in town for a meeting on November 5, and that night he decided that he would go to her meeting–in a wheelchair if necessary.

He wrote down his thoughts at this difficult time.

"I am being faced with death again. I certainly did not invite this intrusion. There is so much I would like to do–so many exciting things in life. But I have no real choice in the matter.

"The tests and treatment seem to get worse as we go along. The spinal taps and injections were terrible, but I made it. I hate this double vision. I look a mess–no hair and one eye covered. But I will fight this thing with the strength of God. I still feel He has much for me to do. I am assured of a great God who comes to me in such times.

"As I look to the past, I can see that God has been good to me. I started with many disadvantages as a child, but God guided me to people who loved and cared. It was from such love that I came to know the love of God in Christ. From there it has been a great life. The greatest thing brought into my life was my dear wife, Nancy. How would I stand these days without her tower of strength? She has always been a source of encouragement in preaching and personal life.

"Right now everything seems to be in holding and I don't like this period. How do you really learn to be patient? I guess I'll have to learn to trust God for every day as well as the great future. 'Teach me, Lord, what it means to live for You today and know Your wholeness for this rough time. You have sustained me so far in everything I have faced. I am amazed because I certainly am not a very courageous person. I used to wonder how others could face such times as this. Now I am finding out what it really is all about.

" 'My continual prayer is that we will soon find the cure to this dreaded disease, cancer. It seems remote to me, but nothing is impossible with You.' "

When I got home, I found the one beautiful bright spot in my day. The women of the church had been over and washed all my windows and cleaned the house! It was another example of their care and love for us.

While Lin was having his private struggles, I was more at peace. I was able to go to bed without weeping. I did not feel hopeless or alone. I wrote that night, "It is great to know that God is your strength; He is with us. But it is also great to have the one you share life with here also share your burden."

Instead of reading Scripture that night, I went through the hymnal, picking out hymns of praise and singing and singing. "For All the Saints" was the hymn that stood out to me. I called Lin in the morning and read the words to him over the phone. And later that day in the hospital, we sang the hymn together, with tears streaming down our faces:

> For all the saints who from their labors rest,
> Who Thee by faith before the world confessed,
> Thy name, O Jesus, be forever blest.
> Alleluia! Alleluia!

Thou wast their rock, their fortress and their might;
Thou, Lord, their captain in the well-fought fight;
Thou, in the darkness drear, their one true light.
Alleluia! Alleluia!

O blest communion, fellowship divine!
We feebly struggle; they in glory shine.
Yet all are one in Thee, for all are Thine.
Alleluia! Alleluia!

And when the strife is fierce, the warfare long,
Steals on the ear the distant triumph song,
And hearts are brave again and arms are strong.
Alleluia! Alleluia!

The golden evening brightens in the west;
Soon, soon to faithful warriors cometh rest;
And sweet the calm of Paradise, the blest.
Alleluia! Alleluia!

But lo! there breaks a yet more glorious day;
The saints triumphant rise in bright array;
The King of Glory passes on His way.
Alleluia! Alleluia!

From earth's wide bounds, from ocean's farthest coast,
Through gates of pearl stream in the countless host,
Singing to Father, Son, and Holy Ghost.
Allelulia! Alleluia! Amen.

William W. How

Reading the words of that hymn and feeling the strength of God again, I decided to begin gathering ideas for Lin's final memorial service, whether it be soon or in fifty years.

I decided that "For All the Saints" just had to be sung. Maybe the choir could sing "To God be the Glory." Someone would have to sing "Complete in Thee," and perhaps "He Giveth More Grace."

And since "Sharing Time" had become such an important part of the life of the church, especially on Sunday nights, I knew Lin would like a sharing time at his final service. Having thought it through, I put the plans aside. I would bring them out sooner than I dreamed.

My mother had said that if I needed her, she would be glad to come back from California and stay with me. I considered this a time of need, and she arrived on Monday, October 30. What a relief that was! I no longer had to run about making arrangements for the care of the boys and the house. It gave the boys and me security and emotional support to have her there and in charge.

Lin was now looking forward to the Kathryn Kuhlman meetings. He was sure one of the doctors would give him a pass to leave the hospital on Sunday afternoon.

But by Wednesday, November 1, Lin's blood count had dropped so low that he was placed in protective isolation. This meant that every visitor had to wear a mask to lessen the spread of germs in his room. To me that seemed an ominous development.

I went home that night and read Psalm 40:1-5:

> I waited, waited for the LORD,
> he bent down to me and heard my cry.
> He brought me up out of the muddy pit,
> out of the mire and the clay;
> he set my feet on a rock
> and gave me a firm footing;
> and on my lips he put a new song,
> a song of praise to our God.
> Many when they see will be filled with awe
> and will learn to trust in the LORD:
> happy is the man
> who makes the Lord his trust,
>
> . . . .

Great things thou hast done,
O LORD my God;
thy wonderful purposes are all for our good;
none can compare with thee;
I would proclaim them and speak of them,
but they are more than I can tell. (NEB)

I went to sleep resting in the goodness of God.

On Thursday morning, Lin's sister, Bonnie Whitten, came from California to visit Lin. She is a nurse and was able to spend several hours a day with her brother.

By Saturday night Lin was still in protective isolation, and it was obvious that he would not be permitted to go to the Kathryn Kuhlman meetings. Bonnie had attended many Kuhlman meetings in California, so we asked her if she could go as Lin's proxy. She was glad to do so.

Bonnie had already written Kathryn Kuhlman about Lin, and so had one of the women in the church. Several had written the Oral Roberts prayer tower, and I personally tried to call Kathryn Kuhlman. I was unable to reach her personally, but was assured of prayer support.

Bonnie went to the meeting but could not get on the platform as Lin's proxy. Several others from Salem also went for the express purpose of praying for healing for Lin. He had to remain in his hospital bed in protective isolation.

Lin had several interns and residents during his many weeks at St. Paul Ramsey Hospital who were concerned about him as a person as well as a patient. Whenever the opportunity arose, Lin would share his commitment to Christ and how his faith had supported him, bringing encouragement and strength. He would lift his hand and say, "*God* is holding my hand." He developed a great concern for many of the nurses and doctors who were uncertain of their faith, or were struggling with life, or who claimed to be agnostic. Many profound discussions were carried on in his room on 7 South at St. Paul Ramsey Hospital.

One resident asked Lin to talk with a woman who had recently been admitted to the hospital with leukemia. This resident, when called to treat a drug-overdose case in the emergency room, said, "It is so hard to realize that there is a man in here, Lindon Karo, who has so much to offer and is fighting for his life, and there are these who want to take their lives."

The doctor had understood how much Lin wanted to live. For about this time Lin wrote, "Most of my thoughts seem to be caught up with the immediate future. I enjoy this life, and I enjoy my family, my friends, the church, the things that are enjoyable in this world."

Meanwhile, Bud DeBar, moderator of the Salem congregation, was struggling with the best method of keeping the people informed of their pastor's condition. The ups and downs came so rapidly, the reasons were so complex, and the prognosis so uncertain, that he hardly knew what to say. The pulpit was being filled with guest speakers, but each Sunday Bud would lead in prayer for Lin and also try to report on his medical condition.

It was not easy. He wanted to be honest without dashing all hope. Lin was receiving many transfusions of blood and of platelets. Members were asked to volunteer blood for the blood bank, to be credited to Lin's account. Many did so.

Both Bud and Lindon had worried what would happen to the church with a pastor who was in the hospital so much of the time, whose strength and future were so uncertain. And how many people wanted to be confronted with death every time they came to church? Perhaps people would stay away simply because they did not want to face suffering and possible death so directly week after week. The congregation was basically young, the vast majority under forty years of age. Many of them had never experienced the death of anyone close to them. How would children and teenagers react to all of this?

But as the weeks and months went by, it was apparent that just the opposite was happening. Attendance grew consistently week after week after week. Even when members and friends did not know whom they would hear preach when they came to church, they kept coming in increasing numbers.

Problems which in other times might have seemed important, seemed insignificant. And as the congregation rejoiced with us over every favorable report on Lindon and wept with every discouraging one, the spirit of love for one another became more all-consuming.

Bud faithfully visited Lin, bringing him up to date on all that was happening at the church, getting his advice and help on decisions that needed to be made concerning church policy, and bringing encouragement from the people.

At this point, Lin was so weak that he could stand only a limited number of visitors. We had found in the earlier days of Lin's hospitalization that some visitors knew how to encourage and help; others made him feel worse. A few visitors suggested that his disease was somehow the punishment of God for sin, either his own or that of the church. This was very difficult for Lin to listen to. He felt that his *disease* was evil. He also saw it as an evil enemy to be fought and conquered if possible. But he did not appreciate people with negative, fatalistic attitudes. So it was announced in church that Lindon would feel free to ask individuals to come when he felt like having visitors. Persons were not to come unless specifically invited. It was a difficult decision to make, but, as usual, the congregation responded with love and understanding. When persons were asked to come, they usually dropped whatever they were doing and came promptly.

One of the men whose visits Lin especially enjoyed was Ralph Cullen. It seemed that Ralph was usually at the hospital when Lin received bad news! In his quiet way, he was of particular help to Lindon. His wife said, "Ralph used to spend his evenings at the health spa. Now he spends them at the hospital with Lindon."

Ralph later commented, "I started out playing tennis with him when he first came to Salem. It was hard now to watch his muscles deteriorating. I had to fight bitterness against God in his illness. But he always made me feel so welcome visiting him; that was just the way he was."

On November 6, Dr. Taddeini came in with additional bad news for Lin. Cancer cells were again appearing in the blood, and he felt helpless to treat it. Lin questioned Dr. Taddeini at length and finally asked him to give a general idea as to how long he might have to live. Dr. Taddeini explained that he could not do that because every person responds differently to the drugs; each case differs from every other case.

Lin was not satisfied. "I want a general idea. Given my set of circumstances and the way I have responded to the drugs and the way my body has reacted thus far, how long do I have—generally?"

The doctor was very reluctant to answer. Finally he said, "Probably a year. Maybe more; maybe less."

It was a tough message to receive.

7

New Hope for Pastor and Church

WITH LIN'S DETERIORATING physical situation and the emotional and spiritual strain upon the church as well as upon our family, the church board felt that some more regular provision should be made for guest speakers and for additional leadership in the church.

The decision was to invite the Rev. Leland Eliason, professor of field education at Bethel Seminary, to become associate pastor of Salem Baptist Church. He would keep his present post at the seminary and add this work to his schedule. It involved being prepared to preach whenever Lin could not be present, and meeting as needed with the church board and church committees. He would do counselling when critically needed. Another seminary teacher, Dr. Clifford Anderson, volunteered to take charge of the calling. Lee had served as pastor of nearby North St. Paul Baptist Church and, since accepting the seminary post, had moved to New Brighton and joined Salem.

In the months ahead he would prove to be a special gift from God to the church and to us at this time. He was not only an excellent speaker, but he was a part of the church body that was sharing the hurts and distress of Lindon's illness.

Lee soon became one of Lin's regular visitors, and from Lee's first visit there was a sense of being soul brothers. Both Lee and Lin enjoyed the writing of Helmut Thielicke, and Lin often saved passages that had been deeply meaningful to him to share with Lee.

Lee later told me about one time when he consulted with Lin about a sermon he was going to preach. "I was preaching on November 5 on 'Focusing on the Right Questions,' from John 21:18-23. I had a very difficult time trying to put it together," Lee said. "Then early that Sunday morning I phoned Lin at the hospital and shared some of my frustration. He listened well and gave me some more ideas and clarification that helped in the sermon."

That sermon had special meaning to many people at Salem, for in it Lee dealt with the questions that he and many of the members were asking, "Why hasn't God healed our pastor?"

After the service, one of the members went home and wrote a letter to Lin about it. Ray Singleton, a student at the seminary, had become very close to us during these months. He had a special gift that Lin needed and appreciated at this time—the gift of humor. An hour with Ray was nearly always an hour of hilarious laughter as Ray rolled off one joke after another. But another side of Ray came through in this letter:

> The sermon this morning was just what I needed. I have really been asking God the wrong questions. . . . In my thirty years as a Christian, I have never enjoyed a pastor like you. You have helped my spiritual life through your preaching and especially because you are a great guy. For the first time in my life I really *enjoy* Bible study and gut-level conversation with God. It surely is great to tell Him that we really don't fully understand Him, but that we really love Him. . . .

> During the past two miserable weeks, I have been stumbling to find answers. I reached out to God with bitterness and almost hate. I was really feeling pity for myself. I looked for comfort and courage to help wipe my tears away, but God's love for us seemed obscured by your illness. But today I could say, Almighty Father, I do love You and I want You to let my life in some small way bear witness to Your sacrifice, kindness, and love to me.
>
> You said that your sermon, if you had preached today, would have been on the love of God. You will never know how much comfort, hope, and encouragement that was to me. The thundering storms and roaring waves suddenly quieted down and I felt peace in the sureness of the fatherhood of God and His unmerited love for me.

Lin was trying to study in preparation for the time he would be back in the pulpit, but he found it very difficult. The eye patch, as well as his overall weakness and pain, bothered him.

His legs were not functioning well now; this was caused by cancer cells being packed in the spinal fluid. To help fight this, the doctors injected Methotrexate, one of the drugs that Lin seemed to respond to, directly into the spinal fluid. It brought a spurt of improvement. His too high white-cell count dropped to a respectable range, and the percentage of malignant cells decreased.

Finally, on November 8, Lin was able to come home, leaving 7 South where he had spent three consecutive weeks. The boys and I were walking on air at the prospect.

He had to come home in a wheelchair and needed assistance to walk. This was hard for him to accept. He was told he would have to return on November 10 for blood tests and x rays. The doctors were especially eager to see how the new drug, Methotrexate, was doing in his system.

Our son Steve's tenth birthday was also November 10,

and I had planned a small party for him right after school. Lin was feeling tired and achy, so he planned to rest after our clinic visit so he would be able to sit in on Steve's party. We arrived at the clinic promptly at 12:30 P.M., our scheduled time, and waited and waited and waited while Lin was feeling sicker and sicker. He was finally seen by a doctor about 3:30, and when he arrived home at 4:30 he was so sick and exhausted he could barely struggle up the stairs to the bedroom. He had to miss the birthday party. It hurt Steve, but it hurt Lin more.

The day after Steve's party, one of my neighbors called. Her son had just returned from Saturday school at the local Catholic parish and he was weeping uncontrollaby. When she was able to get the story out of him, he told her that his teacher, a nun, had been giving a lesson on prayer and concern for others. The nun told of a conversation she overheard at the supermarket between a lady and the checkout clerk concerning a local pastor who had cancer. She had said that only the intervention of God could make this pastor live and continue his preaching ministry. So the nun and her nine-year-old students had a prayer meeting that morning for Lin, asking God to heal him. My neighbor's son had come home crying, "Is that Stevie's daddy we were praying for? Is he going to die? Will God heal him?"

That was one of many prayer meetings in groups and churches of many denominations on behalf of Lin. Each one was a great encouragement to us.

On November 12, the Rev. Warren Magnuson, executive secretary of the Baptist General Conference, spoke at the morning worship hour. Lin was able to attend and lead the service, although he was in much pain and had trouble with muscle coordination. Dr. Magnuson told how the 600 churches of the conference had been alerted to Lin's illness and all were praying for his healing. It lifted our spirits.

It was a full day, with many visitors. When it was over, Lin had a hard time falling asleep. He was again struggling with the problem of life and death. It was not that he was afraid, but rather that he felt such a need to stay and minister.

And I was having my own battles. I lay in bed thinking, *God, why would You want him with You when he could do so much for You here?*

The next morning I awoke with a different attitude. I felt I could say with James, "Count it all joy . . . when you encounter various trials" (1:2).

My mother stayed with us until November 15. She and Lin had a rare son-in-law—mother-in-law relationship that was very meaningful to both of them. He dreaded her leaving as much as I did.

On November 13 and 14, Lin was feeling somewhat better, so she volunteered to stay with the children while Lin and I took two days alone in a hotel with indoor pool, sauna, and whirlpool. They were two great relaxing, refreshing days for both of us.

Among our dear friends for several years were Dan and Nancy Baumann. Dan had been a teacher at Bethel Seminary while Lin was a student, and he had now taken a church in California. About this time, in response to several letters from Dan, Lin wrote to him:

> Although this experience has been difficult physically, Nancy and I have learned a great deal spiritually. My preaching has taken on a new dimension of sharing. I have found that I enjoy preaching even more. Boy, do I miss being away from the people of God when in the hospital. It is hard for me to believe that God would close my ministry here now. . . . Stand with me in prayer that this evil disease will be defeated. I surely want to carry on in the ministry.

The next Sunday was a very special day in the life of Salem Baptist Church. The new sanctuary was to be dedicated, the culmination of several years of work and planning. There were meetings to attend, last-minute preparations, and Lin wanted to be in on everything. With the aid of several men and much encouragement from the congregation, he was able to participate in some of it. On Friday, November 17, there was an organ recital, dedicating the new organ, and also the dedication of a lovely brass plaque made by Dr. Jay Kain, and placed in the narthex of the church. It depicted the four right relationships—with God, with one's self, with the other significant persons in one's life, and with the world—that Lin had so often stressed in his messages since coming to Salem in August, 1971. For the dedicatory brochure, Lin wrote a few paragraphs expressing his feeling about his ministry and that of the church at that time:

> We are grateful to God that we can come to this time in the history of Salem Baptist Church. We are indeed blessed people, for we have ventured out by faith and now we see the fruits of our labors in this new sanctuary of worship. We do not always have the opportunity to see the results of faith so quickly. We have seen the building go up, and we have also seen God fill it with people. Because God is continually sending us new people to help in the ministry and to be ministered to, we cannot look back, but, rather, we must continue to look ahead with the same faith that gave birth to this work.
>
> Let us pray that we will be sensitive to our Lord's guidance, for He has gone ahead of us and has prepared these things. We want those under the tyrannical rule of sin to find the freedom of God's Kingdom. We want the lonely to find the friendly people of God. We want the disillusioned to find the hope of God. We want the people of

> God to find the direction of God through worship. It is for these reasons that we have built this sanctuary.
>
> I believe that serving as the pastor of Salem Baptist Church is the highest privilege in our Baptist General Conference. Never have I seen such dedication, intelligence, stewardship, compassion, discipline, flexibility, and training assembled in one congregation. We are therefore reminded that where much is given, much is required. Let us together move forward into the future that God has for us, using the gifts of the people of God.

The theme of "we cannot look back, we can only move forward" was becoming more and more familiar to my ears. He was using it in many references. But to me the forward look was fraught with questions and sometimes with fear.

Lin led the dedicatory service, leaning heavily on the pulpit as he did so, but he was standing. The dedicatory sermon was given by the Reverend Emmett Johnson, executive secretary of the Minnesota Baptist Conference. He had become a dear friend and a frequent visitor of Lin's during the many weeks of hospitalization. The Salem choir sang "Eternal Life" by Olive Dungan, a musical setting of the words by Saint Francis of Assisi that had now become Salem's regular benediction, repeated in unison by the congregation at the close of each morning service.

> Lord, make me an instrument of Your peace.
> Where there is hatred, let me sow love ;
> where there is injury, pardon;
> where there is doubt, faith;
> where there is despair, hope;
> where there is darkness, light;
> and where there is sadness, joy.
>
> O Divine Master, grant that I may not so much seek to be consoled as to console;
> to be understood as to understand;

to be loved as to love;
for it is in giving that we receive;
it is in pardoning that we are pardoned;
it is in dying that we are born
  to eternal life.

Lin had looked forward to this day for so long, and now, weary but rejoicing in the goodness of God, he had seen it completed.

November 26 Lindon was back in the pulpit for the first time since October 15. He was thrilled to be there, but my heart ached as I watched him. He needed assistance to get to the platform; his suit coat hung loosely on his fragile frame, and his face was ashen in color. But he *was* there in the pulpit.

The hardest part for him was to sit to preach. His usual style was to walk briskly about the platform as he spoke. At first he had suggested a stool on which he could sit. But in discussing this with Bud DeBar, church chairman, they both realized it would take considerable energy to stay seated on a stool. So the pulpit was moved and a table and chair put in its place. Bud told Lin, "You always wanted a Spurgeon's preaching rail. You may be the first to make the 'Karo Table' famous." That lifted Lin's spirits and he sat at the table to preach his sermon on, "Crucified, Dead, and Buried."

Bud DeBar later commented about that table, "It kept him in one spot. It seemed to bring him in close to the people, and he was able to relax and gesture very effectively. But it was such a contrast to what he would have chosen. The last few months of his life were totally the opposite of what he would have wanted. But he probably did more in those few months than many do in a lifetime of ministry.

"It was an opportunity that few of us will ever have—to sit under a man who has the word that he is going to die—

humanly speaking—or that his chances of living are slim. Yet this man felt that his intense desire, even unto death, was to preach at the sacrifice of everything else, even his life. To stay in the hospital was the worst thing that could happen, but he could tolerate it six days a week. But never on Sunday. His one desire was to preach, to communicate with people.

"Despite his physical weakness, the church continued to grow. At this time, the petty things that often surface in a church were put aside, and instead, the people wrapped around the Karo family."

As Lin spoke, the rest of his body was obviously deteriorating, but his voice retained its usual vigor.

* * *

Crucified, Dead, and Buried

Yes, I'm going to *sit* and preach today.
I like to move around the platform as I speak,
but I have no choice.
I can't stand that long.

Perhaps I approach the subject of the crucifixion with a bit of fear.
I am not superstitious,
but my last sermon to you five weeks ago
was that Christ suffered under Pontius Pilate.
I felt good that Sunday. But Monday morning I began suffering and it went on for the next three weeks.
I hope today's message is not prophetic of what is to come: crucified, dead, and buried!

If we are to accept the crucifixion of Jesus Christ,
we must accept a concept of God
that may jolt us a bit.

Most of us prefer to think that God is always kind,
and always doing good things for us.
But the crucifixion shouts
that everything is *not* right in this world,
and that God takes the waywardness of men seriously.
We like to think about Jesus as compassionate,
concerned about others.
But why should Jesus die on a cross?
How does that provide salvation?
We can't see why that had to be part of the plan of God.

People have many explanations for Jesus' death.
Some see Jesus as a Victim of circumstances.
He came into an historic situation
that was not ready for Him politically and culturally,
and He got crucified.
Other people toy with the idea that the crucifixion
was an example of what happens to good people—
they get crucified.

But the biblical account does not support these ideas.
It says there is something wrong with men,
that we are all sinners.
It is 2,000 years
since a group of people crucified Christ.
But the hatred and greed and lust of Jesus' day
are in every heart.

The crucifixion reveals the hatred and insensitivity of people.
When a person in Jesus' time was convicted of crime,
he was scourged with a long leather thong
studded with nails and pieces of bone
and sharpened pellets of lead.
It was so brutal that many persons collapsed
or died from the scourging.
In the trial of Jesus, Pilate ordered Him to be scourged
before he pronounced Him guilty,

hoping this would win the sympathy of the people (see Luke 23:22).
After scourging, a criminal would be compelled
to carry his own cross to the place of execution.
There he would be stripped of his clothing
and nailed or tied to the cross.
The worst torture involved
the span of time a man might hang on that cross.
Terrible infections and fever usually set in.
A man could hang in torture on the cross
as long as a week waiting to die.
In the crucifixion of Jesus,
death mercifully came soon.

When we look at such details,
remember that man's *sin* made the cross possible.
But the cross reveals not only our sin
but also God's infinite love.
The cross says that although I may stomp on God,
and kick God, God still was willing to *die* for me.
Through the cross, God says,
"That's how much you are worth.
That's how much I love you."
Sometimes we get involved with theological terms
about the cross—atonement, substitution, justice, etc.
God is not concerned with our terms.
God says, "How much do I love people?
I *died* for them."

Since I have had cancer
there have been at least a half a dozen people
in this congregation who have said to me,
"Pastor, I wish I could take your place.
I wish it were possible for me to have what you have
so that you could have my good health."
And those people meant it.
What an expression of love!

But those people may not really know *me.*
They know me only as a concerned pastor.
  But *God* truly knows me.
He knows what kind of a person I am inside,
  and God still says,
"I love you so much I died for you."

I am going home this afternoon
and watch TV as the Vikings play.
I hope I'll see Fran Tarkenton throw a touchdown pass;
and if he does, I'm going to hoot and holler.
  But this morning I sit here
and tell you calmly that God died for me.
  I ought to be shouting in excitement.
Sometimes I say to myself, "What is wrong with me?
  God *died* for me. God cares!"

The idea that God died for men
  was hard for the early Church to comprehend.
  The early Church lived in a society
  that held to the Greek gnostic concept that all matter,
    including the body, was evil.
  The early Church had to go against the Greek teaching
  of its time to believe that God could take on a
    human body and *die.*

One of the early heresies held that the true God
  left the body of Jesus before the crucifixion.
  Only thus could He remain "pure"
  and therefore spiritual and good.
    I'm glad that the Bible teaches
  that God identified Himself *fully* with us in Jesus Christ.
  God is not waving to me from heaven, saying,
    "Lindon Karo, in all of the disease
  you've got in your body, good luck."
  Instead, I have a God who has identified Himself with me
  to the ultimate limit—death itself—
    so that I may be forgiven.

What is the forgiveness of God?
If you wrong me and ask forgiveness,
and I say lightly, "That's all right, buddy;
don't worry about it,"
I am not taking seriously your sin against me.
But when God died for us He took our sin seriously.
He says,
"I know what resentment and hatred are really like
because I have been tempted in every way as you are.
I faced death like you.
I am your Brother; I stand beside you."

How do I know that God forgives me?
Because He *died* for me.
Colossians 2:13-14 says,

> And you, who were dead in trespasses and the uncircumcision of your flesh, God made alive together with him, having forgiven us all our trespasses, having canceled the bond which stood against us with its legal demands; this he set aside, nailing it to the cross (RSV).

Paul says the crucifixion not only reveals your sin
and the love of God,
but also reveals justice,
victory,
something made right.
And the words
"Having canceled the bond which stood against us
with its regal demands"
mean that you wrote, as in your own handwriting,
your sins, and now they stand against you.
Paul says that the autograph
detailing your sins against you has been canceled,
that although God has a signed confession from us
the crucifixion has erased it.
Colossians 2:13 says, "When we stand before God,
Christ says our sin is canceled.

We are persons who have been made right
by what Christ has done."

Verse 15 is beautiful:

> When He had disarmed the rulers and authorities, He made a public display of them, having triumphed over them through Him.

The cross that was the scandal of history
became victory for all men
and has defeated the forces of evil.
We don't have to be defeated by the powers of sin.
God says we no longer have to live
in our natural self-centeredness,
but, rather, there is a full new life
for the people of God to enjoy.
Through the cross we have become the people of God.

Why didn't God do it differently?
Why didn't Jesus come in all of His glory and power
and just roll the people before Him?
I'm glad He came as He did,
for He knows fully what I am going through *right now.*
If you have never faced real suffering
or unsolvable problems,
you may not appreciate that Christ came as He did,
not with pomp and glory,
not demanding that men fall down before Him,
but as a human being like you.
When you face the crunch,
Christ's suffering and death carry meaning.

But Christ's crucifixion, death, and burial
are not the end of the story. He rose again.
The resurrected Christ is here
and He offers to us a new kind of life
of relationship to Himself.

What is your basic sin?
It is self-centeredness and abstraction from life.
If you don't know Christ,
you don't really love that person next to you,
for you have never experienced the love that God had
when He died for mankind.
When we enter into fellowship with Christ,
life is no longer abstract; people become real;
God becomes real; we experience a fullness of life
despite our circumstances and problems.

But you must make it operative
by trusting Him as your Saviour and Lord.
Right now life would be hopeless for me without Him,
but God has grabbed ahold of my heart
and has shown me a new kind of life with Him.

* * *

After the service, more than a dozen young people whom Lin had not seen before were standing in the line to shake hands with him. They were from Salem Covenant Church, about a mile from our church. One young man identified himself as the youth director of the church. He told Lin, "Twenty of us have covenanted to pray daily for you, and we have been doing so for several weeks. Because our interest in you is so deep, we wanted to come and hear you speak. We just want you to know that we love you and will continue to pray." Lin was deeply moved.

I later learned that those young people had gone back to their own church that evening and shared the experiences they had in our morning service. As a result, the entire service turned into a sharing time and prayer service for Lin.

8

December Joy and Despair

ON DECEMBER 3, Lin preached the most difficult sermon he had ever prepared, based on the words in the Apostles' Creed, "He Descended into Hell." Scholars disagree on the interpretation of this phrase, and he probably spent more time in preparation on this sermon than on any other in the series, with the possible exception of the first.

* * *

He Descended into Hell

This phrase in the Apostles' Creed,
"He descended into hell,"
has been one about which I have had many questions.
But in studying the history of the Apostles' Creed,
I found that many others have struggled with it, too.
When the creed was being formulated,
some didn't want to include it.
Others thought it did not really refer to hell.
But by the fifth century most students of Scripture
seemed to agree that Christ *did* descend into hell.

Most of us don't like to talk about hell.
We prefer to talk and think about heaven.

Christians have been criticized for being
pie-in-the-sky people because we seem
more interested in some beautiful future
than in the world around us.
Perhaps our problem is that we have interpreted heaven
only as a future place.
But if we have been criticized
about our attitude toward heaven,
it is as nothing compared to the ridicule
that has been heaped on us
regarding our teachings about hell.

We are people who take seriously the teaching of the Bible,
and therefore we cannot ignore the subject of hell.
The Bible frequently talks about hell,
and the teaching that Christ descended into hell
is very important.
It means that God invaded hell itself
and *that* is *good news.*

Something wonderful happened because He descended into hell.
First Peter 3:18-20 says,

> For Christ also died for sins once for all, the just for the unjust, in order that He might bring us to God, having been put to death in the flesh, but made alive in the spirit; in which also He went and made proclamation to the spirits now in prison, who once were disobedient, when the patience of God kept waiting in the days of Noah, during the construction of the ark, in which a few, that is, eight persons, were brought safely through the water.

Although this is a difficult passage, two things seem clear.
First, Christ was put to death.
Second, He went and preached to the spirits in prison
who once were disobedient
when the patience of God kept waiting in the days of Noah.

Peter is saying that Christ went to a place
where He preached to people
who before had not obeyed the message they had heard
from Noah.
I think Peter is zeroing in on a particular people.
The passage seems to state that Christ
went to the place where all these people were,
and He preached to them.
What did He preach? He probably proclaimed
the Good News about the Kingdom of God.
This raises many questions.
Why did Jesus, after His earthly ministry,
go to hell
and preach the Good News there?
What did He hope to accomplish?
Although we cannot fully answer these questions,
His going tells us something about the whole event
of Christ's coming,
His death, and what God intended to do.
Just think, even hell was not left out of that message!
We don't know what happened to those listeners.
But His going there reveals another truth
about the kind of Saviour we have.
It tells us that God is compassionate.
Even those who formerly had not heard of this Christ,
or who had been disobedient, were not left out.

Christ, who was concerned for those people,
has the same concern for me.
Regardless of the kind of personal "hell" I may have created
in my own life-style, Christ still loves me
and is concerned about me.
If you feel, "I am the kind of person
who can't be reached by God,"
remember that Christ descended into hell
to make the Good News known.

Now if He went to that extent,
how far would He go to reach you?
There is no person who is unreachable by Christ.
No other religion brings a message saying,
"God so loved people that He became a part of humanity
and was crucified, died, buried,
and went to that humanity's hell."

Now, when we talk about hell,
what are we really talking about?
Jesus used many expressions to describe hell (Luke 8:12).
He said there is gnashing of teeth,
perhaps signifying the anxiety of knowing
you missed the purpose of life.
He also described hell as outer darkness,
the realization of hopelessness.
In other places, hell is said to be
burning and torment,
a description of knowing no forgiveness.
All these are vivid descriptions of hell.

When we put all of these metaphors together,
what do they describe? What is Christ saying?
He is saying that hell is separation from God.
Hell becomes a way of life that you start here,
and it ends up being your permanent state.
Jesus said He came to give life and to give it abundantly.
He was talking about heavenly life
as compared to hellish life.
To follow Christ
means to come alive to God and to people.

How do we become alive to one another?
Jesus said, "You gave Me a cup of cold water.
You saw Me as a person.
You clothed Me.
You saw Me in need."

Christ said He came to give us this new life,
and it delivers us from self-centered living.
That is what life is all about.

The isolated self is the hell-bound self.
Only Christ can deliver us
from our self-centered, independent life
that will eventually leave us
forsaken, forever separated from God.

What happens when a person dies?
What happens to me when I die?
The Scriptures assure me that death for the believer
is not a dreadful experience with a terrible sting.

Death has a different connotation for me
because Christ descended into hell.
The sting of death is the mystery,
the uncertainty of it all.
But death is foreign to what God wanted in His creation.
In the story of Adam and Eve,
we see that sin limited mankind.
Adam and Eve, like all of us,
wanted to become supermen. We wanted to be infinite,
to go beyond the bounds that God has prescribed for us.
Adam and Eve disobeyed God,
and God made them—and us—finite
by making all of us experience death.
You are going to die. So am I.
I probably have been reminded of it
more often recently than you have.

How do I face death?
I have found a Saviour who holds my hand.
And I know that in my dying moments
Christ will continue to hold my hand.

How do I know? Because Christ loved me so much
that He died, was buried, descended into hell, and
preached the Good News even there.
Since He descended into hell
and vanquished the forces of evil,
I have nothing to fear.
He has opened up the fullness of life for me,
and He is holding my hand today.

However, I must say
that the emphasis of the Bible is on the *now.*
Today is the day of salvation.
We prepare for the future by living for the present.
That is very important to me.
I may have a year, a few months, a few weeks;
but I will live fully today,
knowing that death will not rob me
of the rich life He has provided for me.

Since I have been ill, Christ has meant more to me,
and there are many things
that are not important to me anymore.
I used to like new suits.
I used to like to think about buying new cars.
But those things are nothing now.
But my relationship to Christ
and my relationship to you are so important
that I can't express them in words.
I think if we would really grasp the truth
of what Christ has done for us,
of who He is and what He does in life,
a lot of priorities would change.

We are transformed by our relationship to God,
and we live for today,
knowing that when the day of death comes,
He will be there to hold our hand.

* * *

Lin still felt fairly well on December 4 when he gave the message "The Crucial Half" at Bethel Seminary Chapel. He was eager to share with prospective pastors some of the lessons he had learned about helping people who are ill, and what he felt were important qualities for a pastor to have.

* * *

The Crucial Half

The Bethel Seminary motto is:
"The Man of God Communicating the Word of God."
I used to think that the most important part
of that motto was "Communicating the Word of God."
But I have discovered in the last four months,
since I learned that I have cancer,
that the most important part is being a "Man of God."

It is great to have men who can give great messages.
But what we need even more
are *men of God.*
One person in the Bible is called
"a man after God's own heart."
Perhaps this man, David, can show us what it means
to be a "man of God."

David respected others. God told David
he was going to become a king.
But there was already a king–Saul–
and Saul was out to kill David.
Yet David had so much respect for Saul
that he refused to hurt him.
David knew something that many of us need to learn:
a reverent respect for other children of God.
That respect must start right here in seminary.
In school we tend to get involved

in climbing the ladder of success.
Good grades in school help us
to get good recommendations and a good church.
Success in that first church helps us to get a better church.
It is easy to start walking over people
on the way to success.
But David, a man after God's own heart,
did not have that attitude toward Saul.

In our day the Holy Spirit is doing some wonderful things,
maybe in churches other than your own.
The work of the Gospel is too big for any one church
in a community,
and God is working today through many channels.
Our own church has great fellowship
with the Lutheran church across the street from us.
That pastor is a man of God
who really preaches the Gospel.
Up the street is Faith Christian Reformed Church,
and we are developing real fellowship with that church.
A few weeks ago, the youth pastor
from Salem Covenant Church, a mile down the road,
was in our church on Sunday morning
with a group of his young people.
He came to me afterward and said,
"I just want you to know that twenty young people
from our church have covenanted together to pray
for your healing."
That is fellowship based on mutual respect.

There are other qualities of David that we should note.
The man of God has confidence in the power of God.
Think back to the story of David and Goliath.
The Israelites were badly frightened
and no one knew what to do.
Then young David came on the scene saying,

"Who does this Goliath think that he is,
that he should mock God?
I'll go out and take care of the situation."
That's confidence in the power of God.

One day in the hospital I got really bad news.
When I had first been diagnosed as having lymphosarcoma,
it looked bad; but the drugs did a terrific job,
and for five weeks I seemed to have a complete arrest.
Then suddenly I developed double vision,
numbness, and other symptoms.
At first the doctors thought it was a reaction to the drugs.
Then they did a spinal tap
and found many malignant cells in the spinal fluid.
This was treated, and the malignant cells seemed to disappear.

While treating me, they were checking my blood each day.
One day the specialist came and told me
that malignant cells were being found
in what they call the peripheral blood.
He said drugs for treating this were very limited
and it would probably be only a time
until I would die.
That news was difficult to take.

Later that evening, Pastor Art Rouner
of Colonial church in Edina came to see me.
He entered quietly.
(It might be well for you to remember
that when a person is very ill,
he doesn't appreciate visitors who come bounding
into his room.
The one thing I want is good health
and if I'm lying there half dead
and a man comes jovially in as if to pat me on the back,

I don't like it.)
Then Rouner asked, "Well, how is it going?"
I told him what the doctor had said that afternoon.

He took my hand and said, "This is not going to happen to you.
I and the men of Colonial church are going to stand
in the gap for you.
You are a servant of God, a chosen vessel,
and God is going to do something in your behalf."
And then he prayed:
"Take the weak faith that I have
and the weak faith of Lindon
and put the two faiths together. Heal him."
He had confidence in the power of God.
That day I needed a man of God and he was one.

Where does that kind of confidence in God come from?
How did David have it?
You'll remember that Goliath was not David's first enemy.
He had already fought a bear and a lion.
Perhaps that is one of the things that is troubling me.
At the age of thirty-two, I'm not sure I've fought a bear
and a lion,
but I know I have a Goliath in front of me right now.

While you are in seminary, there are bears and lions to face,
but you can avoid them by not getting involved with people.
But you had better wrestle with those bears
and lions right now
so that when you visit someone in the hospital,
you can take him by the hand and say,
"Listen, I know God, and God is bigger
than this whole situation you are facing,
and I'm not going to let you go."

Another quality that stands out in a real man of God
is his honesty.

It is probably the honesty of the psalms
that keeps us coming back to them.
David didn't hesitate to express how he really felt
about himself, about God, and about the world
in which he lived. But in the psalms,
we also see David grabbing hold of God.

One layman in our church has been of real help to me.
He is so confident that God is going to heal me.
Yet almost every time he has visited me
it has been on days when I have gotten bad news.
One day he told me about a sermon
that had been preached in my absence. He said,
"He talked about the struggles we face
when we think about someone dying.
It hit me squarely, for when I left here
the day after you had received such bad news,
I had said to my wife,
'I'm afraid I'm going to become a bitter man.' "

Strangely enough, that helped me,
for I knew that here was a man who really loved me
and who was honest with me and with God.

I could say a lot about people who have visited me
in the hospital. Some have come to preach,
with their three points all lined up
and with all the answers.
They were no help.

I preferred the visitors who, like David,
could honestly express their frustrations
and still lay hold of God in confidence.
When you are in trouble, what you want is a man of God.

* * *

Lin was consuming many pints of blood and platelets

from the blood bank. Later in December the Red Cross Blood Bank came to the seminary, and ninety-one Bethel seminary students, student wives, and faculty members volunteered to give a pint of blood to be credited to his account. Twenty-three volunteers were rejected for minor medical reasons, but sixty-eight pints were given.

Soon after his seminary chapel talk Lin began to have sharp shooting pains in his left leg; they were so severe that he could not stand. The numbness in his lower lip and fingers became pronounced, and he was unable to button or unbutton his shirts.

On December 7, he was readmitted to the hospital for the third time. When I returned home that night from the hospital, I was deeply discouraged. I prayed a lot that night and slowly began to realize more fully that the power of God is available to us if we ask. My prayers became more positive than ever before.

The next day I was driving and had the three boys with me. I explained to them that God is powerful and that we should claim that power as we pray. "Let's pray definitely that Daddy will be healed," I said.

Scotty, now three, yelled, "Yippee! Then I can ride on his back!"

Another series of tests began, but nothing new was revealed.

Lee went up to see Lin as soon as he heard that he had been readmitted to the hospital. "I don't remember exactly how the conversation started," he later recalled, "but I soon found myself telling Lin some of my frustrations in my seminary work, that I didn't seem to really have in-depth relationships with the students. He listened very carefully, and then he cautiously began passing on some of the comments seminary men had given him regarding their impressions of me. He put his finger precisely on what the real problem was. I left thinking, *I was supposed to come to cheer him up and minister to him, but he served the pastor role to me and gave me great help.* I found that I was not the only one to whom he was ministering in his hospital bed. Even when the pressure of his illness weighed heavily, he would hear what somebody else was saying and put himself into their situation."

We were all relieved when he was released on Saturday, December 9. I wanted so much for us to have a happy Christmas together. In the back of my mind was always the gnawing thought, *Is this the last one?*

Lin had originally intended to have a special Advent series of messages before Christmas, but with the uncertainties of his hospital visits, the chemotherapy that interrupted his sermons, and his desire to finish his series on the Apostles' Creed, he decided to continue with this series.

Our plans were short-lived. On Sunday, the day after he was released, he developed intense pains in his left arm. He was unable to preach. To add to his disappointment, the Salem choir Christmas concert was scheduled for the evening, and Lin was in such pain that he could not attend.

Since I sang in the choir, and Lin and the boys knew how much it meant to me, Steve volunteered to stay home with his dad. The pain was so severe that Lin often cried out. Steve later told me, "Dad would scream because it hurt so much. I didn't know what to do but he was glad I was here, and I was so glad I could help Dad."

The pain decreased on Monday, but because it was still present, he was again admitted to the hospital on Wednesday, December 13. Tests showed his white blood-cell count was increasing, with a larger percentage of malignant cells present. To fight the growing number of malignant cells, he was given an injection of the drug Methotrexate directly into the spinal fluid. His platelet count was decreasing.

Platelets are essential for the blood to clot, and a too low count increases the danger of internal hemorrhaging. On Friday he had a transfusion of platelets.

A new intern, Dr. Dave Opsahl, was on the floor now. Lin was impressed with his skill. Spinal taps had been very painful, but he was able to perform them with little pain. They developed a deep friendship, and Dave spent many hours with Lin. He would come in whenever he could spare a few moments, and they would discuss his case, the significance of each blood count, etc., as well as politics and other matters. And Lin would share with everyone who seemed interested his "adventure with God in dying"—that is what he called it. Dave obviously cared for Lin as a person and friend as well as a patient. Knowing how much it meant to Lin to be able to preach, Dave worked to help him get a pass from the hospital so he could preach on Sunday.

On Sunday, December 17, both Dr. Dave Opsahl, Lin's intern, and Dr. Luigi Taddeini, his specialist, were in the service. Lin spoke on "Christ Rose Again from the Dead."

* * *

Christ Rose Again from the Dead

I have been waiting a long time to get to this
part of the Apostles' Creed.
If you think I'm going to make the resurrection
have an application to the Advent season,
you're exactly right, because I think
the Advent season shows the ultimate
in God's action on behalf of man.

God acted in creation;
He acted in giving us special revelation, the Word of God;
He acted through the prophets;

and finally He acted
in the incarnation and coming of Jesus Christ.
In Christ's life, death, and resurrection,
He did something for all of us
that we could not do for ourselves.
The resurrection marks the beginning
of a new creation of God.

I have another reason for being eager
to preach on the resurrection.
Right after I preached on "Suffered Under Pontius Pilate"
I had a series of setbacks, and I suffered so much
I began to wonder if my sermons were becoming prophetic.
If so, I want to rush on to the resurrection.
I hope that I soon will begin to gain new strength.
I'm only out on a weekend pass this morning,
so tomorrow I have to go back to the hospital.
I'm very thankful that my doctors are here this morning.
I don't know if they figured I might need help,
but I'm glad they are here this morning worshiping with us.

To understand the resurrection, we must understand both
death and life.
People who face death today
sometimes talk about "the glorious day
when I'm going to be released from my body."
That is *not* what Jesus taught.
Jesus taught a unity between body and soul.
When we get really sick,
we find how impossible it is to separate body and soul.
They are intrinsically connected.
That's the key to understanding what Jesus came to do.
Jesus struggled with death because death is an enemy.

Look at Jesus Christ in the Garden of Gethsemane.
We see a man, thoroughly human,
begging His disciples, "Don't go to sleep.

I'm soon to die, and I don't want to be alone."
Jesus Christ does *not* say, "Here's My glorious moment."
Instead, He says, "Father, if it is possible,
remove this cup from Me. I don't want to drink it.
Nevertheless, not My will but Yours" (see Mark 14:36).

Jesus knew that death destroys the God-created life
that He intended to be good.
True, the soul does not die at physical death,
but the resurrection is concerned with the *whole* man,
a new act of creation.

How did death come about if God never intended it?
Why do I have a disease
that will eventually take my life?
Why does everyone face death someday?
Jesus saw death as an enemy
that has come because of man's problem of sin.
The Genesis account tells us
that death is a curse, foreign to the plan of God.
Death cannot be removed until sin is removed.
Once we understand this, we can see
that the resurrection is a bigger concept
than that of Jesus rising on the third day.

We all want to be superhuman, independent of God.
Therefore death came to remind us
that we are not superhuman, that our lives are limited.
Every man, woman, and child here will *die*.
Death reminds all of us
that we need Someone beyond ourselves.
We cannot truly live without God.
Christ came to do something about the problem of death.
Death is an alien, corrupting force.

The Bible uses the word "flesh,"
but it does not mean our body cells.

It means the corruption that entered the world with sin.
Corruption includes our deceit,
our self-centeredness,
our inability to really see people.
Corruption also takes the form of disease and death.
Christ in His coming sets a new force into operation
that the Bible calls the force of the Spirit.
Paul often writes about the Spirit and the flesh.
Flesh is the power of death.
Spirit is the power of life, God's power of creation.
Paul says these two powers are at war in this world.
The New Testament envisions
both body and spirit as originally good,
but now fallen under the deadly power of flesh or corruption.
They must be set free by the power of the Holy Spirit.
Christ came to release this new power, to begin a new age.
The resurrection of Christ
was the start of the rolling back of corruption.

Jesus looked at death as an enemy to be destroyed.
Therefore Christ had to enter into this stronghold Himself
and experience death. But that is not the end.
To understand the resurrection,
we must understand not only death, but also life.

Usually we associate the resurrection
with the day when Christ will come back
and everybody will be resurrected.
But the New Testament does not make that jump.
It says the resurrection
is to be experienced *now* in our lives.
God can work in your life right now,
and you can be a part of God's Kingdom, God's rule.
The Bible makes it clear
that if you are not experiencing that new spirit kind
of creation,

you probably will not experience resurrection life
beyond the grave.

In Luke 24 we have the story of two men
walking along a road
talking about the dramatic events that had occurred.
Christ was walking with them,
but they did not recognize Him. Why?
They had all the facts correct. He was gone from the tomb;
the angels told the women this.
But they were caught up with talking about events
rather than experiencing the Person.

We all tend to fall into that same trap.
Search out all the historical information
about the resurrection, and what do we have?
A stack of facts.
Would that really help anyone?
It is only the *experience* of Christ
that transforms life.
The resurrection tells us
that every person can have a living relationship with God.
In the story of the disciples on the way to Emmaus,
the change came when they invited Him to share their lives.
They sat down and broke bread together.
It is in the breaking of the bread of daily living
that Christ becomes real.

Who is the Christ who helps me face this cancer?
It is not a Christ who was just a great man
who lived on this earth. It is not even the Christ
who wears a crown and is a king.
Rather, it is the Christ who suffered for me,
who knows what suffering is.
It is the Christ who not only died for me,
but who also was resurrected and lives
to bring me through my valley of the shadow of death.

He gives a new power to face these days.
He gives me purpose for living.
I need and you need the God
who is rolling back the forces of evil,
and who is at work in this world.

One character in Scripture for whom I am thankful is Thomas.
Thomas just couldn't believe in the resurrection.
He was not with the rest of the disciples
the first time Jesus appeared to them.
When they told him that Christ was alive,
he said, "That is impossible. That can't be."
He said, "Unless I can take my own hand
and put it in His wounds, I'm not going to believe you."
The next time Jesus appeared before the disciples,
Thomas was with them.
Jesus said, "Come and put your hand in the wound."
Thomas fell before Him and said, "My Lord and my God."
I used to think he did this
because he saw the wounds and therefore believed.
I don't think that anymore.
Rather, I think Thomas recognized Jesus
as One who loved and understood him
despite his doubts and problems.

That's the wonder of Christ.
Whatever problem or doubt you face,
Christ keeps coming to you, saying,
"I love you and I want you to experience Me.
This relationship will bring a new experience
with the Holy Spirit.
He will give you power to see the corruption of sin
and to be an instrument of Mine to push it back
and to come alive to the Spirit."

You may ask, "Why should I need
the power of the Holy Spirit? I'm doing all right."

But every one of us is trapped in his own prison
of self-centered, independent living.
It takes the power of the resurrection
to deliver a man from that.
That power begins to work when we say,
"I need Christ to release me from my style of life
and open my eyes to a new style of life."

Christ can make us instruments of God
in this process of new creation.
The Church is called the Body of Christ.
The world may ask, "Where is the resurrected Christ?"
The resurrected Christ is in the midst of His people,
His Body.
Christ started something in His resurrection
that I call the new age, the new work of the Spirit.
We become for others a mediating presence of Christ.
If this new age is embodied in His people,
then the world has a right to ask,
"Where are the scars? Where is the love, the compassion?"
We have a great responsibility.
What are we doing with the Holy Spirit
that God has given us? The new age?
The resurrected Christ in our midst?

God is moving His drama forth,
and there is coming a great day of resurrection
when there will no longer be cancer or other diseases.
I don't understand what that day will be like,
but the Bible indicates we're pushing toward it.
The resurrection of Christ points to it;
the Church points to it.
People are being transformed by His Spirit.

You can experience that resurrected Christ
by committing yourself to Him.

* * *

Sunday evening Lin had to return to the hospital. Ralph and Nancy Cullen went with us, and on the way we stopped at a restaurant for a bite to eat. With Ralph's help, Lin could get to and from the car. By now, every apparently small event, such as a sandwich in a restaurant, was a particular joy.

When I got home that night, I wrote in my diary how I felt.

"I'm sick of lallygagging around. I want to mean business with You, God. Let's get Satan out of here and back to where he belongs—in hell. Let's give You the glory and claim victory. I don't care whose prayers are answered—those who can only focus on healing and not on You, or those concerned with Your will who say they don't really know how to pray. We've all struggled with this so much that we get wishy-washy in our prayer. Here's what I want: Lin's complete healing, back to his normal strength, yet with the same zeal he has for You now. Thank You, God. No room for doubts tonight."

On Monday more tests were run, showing that his white count had decreased considerably. Another injection of Methotrexate was given.

On Thursday, December 21, he was released from the hospital on the condition that he would come to the clinic daily for blood counts and further injections as needed. Just before he was released he was to have another platelet transfusion. Because of the shortage of fresh blood during December, we had to wait and wait and wait. I had asked Ray Singleton, a seminary student and friend, to come with me because I knew I would need assistance in getting Lin in and out of the car.

During that long wait for the platelet transfusion, Ray began bringing out his lively repertoire of jokes. No matter what topic Lin mentioned, Ray had jokes on hand. We all laughed until we ached. The nurses finally came and shut our door, saying that it was catching and they were becoming silly at the nursing station. Ray turned what would have been a frustrating afternoon into a highly enjoyable time.

Almost all of Lin's time was consumed in battling his disease. He struggled hard to prepare his sermons for the times when he would be able to preach. But he could do nothing else as far as the church was concerned, and this bothered him.

During one of Lee Eliason's visits, Lin shared his sense of guilt with Lee. Lee told him, "Your ministry cannot be measured in terms of the hours you spend with the church but on the impact and influence you are having. You are ministering in a powerful way through your illness." He told Lin that the amazing part of his messages was that although he freely referred to his illness, he never did it in a way to create self-pity but, rather, to illustrate the truth of God's Word in a given situation.

This concept of his ministry was reinforced when one of the mothers in the church shared a theme that her eighth-grade daughter, Kathi Erickson, had written in school.

* * *

A Radical Change

Cancer is a sad thing. I hope so much that soon a miracle drug will be found, a drug that can cure all cancer. A few years back my grandpa died from cancer. It was sad because I loved him, but I've pretty much gotten over it now.

Like I said, cancer is a sad thing, no matter who it hits. But in this case, it's especially sad.

It all started late last August. All the junior high kids

from church were piled in the bus heading for dear old Trout Lake Camp.

After many long, loud hours on the road, we finally reached the campgrounds. Then we went through the usual routine of waiting impatiently in the long lines, first, to have your throat checked by the camp nurse and, second, to find out what cabin you'd be in. The lines seemed to move faster when we'd meet some of our senior high friends who had spent the past week there at Trout and were leaving that day. They were envied by us junior high kids because their camp pastor had been Pastor Karo, the minister of our church. We all really liked him.

Pastor was a young, good-looking man of thirty-one. He had black hair. His brown eyes were framed by gold-rim glasses. And he was one fantastic pastor! But while he had been up at camp he hadn't felt too good. He thought he had the flu or something.

Getting back to camp, Linda, Corrie, Chris, and I were all in the same cabin, White Pine. Linda, a well-tanned blonde, was Catholic and had come to Trout with Chris. Corrie was a little on the short side, with long, dark hair and a freckly face. Chris, then a little overweight, had some freckles too and bright blue eyes. Her hair was short and very blonde. She wore wire-frame glasses. She and Corrie were two of my closest friends, along with Kim. But Kim was in another cabin with other friends of hers.

Well, time passed, and we were having a great time, except for one little thing. One guy from our church had gotten a letter from home. It said Pastor was in the hospital from a blood clot. I prayed for him and tried not to think about it.

A day or two later, after my first Bible class, I started walking back to the cabin.

"Kathi!"

I turned around and saw Chris walking toward me.

"Kathi, I was in my Bible class, and Pastor Lind started talking about a young minister he knew that just found out he had cancer. So when he was done, I asked him who this guy was. It's Pastor Karo."

"You're kidding!" I didn't know what to say or think, so I stared at the ground in shock. My face grew hot and my eyes began to sting. The ground below me grew blurred and fuzzy as the tears flowed down my cheeks.

Just then Corrie walked up to us. I started to blurt out everything I'd just heard, but she stopped me.

"I know, I know. Pastor Hogan talked about him, too." Then she began crying.

"C'mon, you guys. We better get to our next class," Chris said unsteadily.

So the three of us, red-eyed and sobbing, started back to the cabin.

That night, all the girls from Salem (our church) tried to get together with the Salem boys to pray for Pastor. The boys couldn't make it, but we had a meeting anyway. God really worked in that circle of prayer. When it was over we had a great feeling of relief. We knew God would take care of everything.

A day or two later, we found out one of our pastor's doctors was Dr. Christenson, Chris's dad. After a lot of hard work, Chris was finally allowed to phone home, to find out more about Pastor.

The news was anything but good. Pastor would die unless some miracle happened.

Then Pastor Swenson talked to Mrs. Christenson over the phone, and we went on to lunch.

That must have been the hardest meal I've ever tried to eat. I kept thinking about Pastor's wife and three sons, and how much I really cared for Pastor. Most of all I kept thinking about all the things that must be running through his mind.

When Pastor Swenson gave the lunch announcements, he had said he wanted to talk to all the Salem kids after lunch on the benches outside the mess hall. So when we had all finished eating, we gathered by the benches. Soon Pastor Swenson showed up.

"Well, as some of you know, Chris called home this morning. She talked to her mom, and the word isn't good. Pastor Karo has cancer. It started in the chest and has spread through his entire body. The truth is, unless the Lord performs a miracle, he'll die."

Though we had all been silent, it suddenly seemed much quieter. Our heads were all turned to the ground. Everyone was crying—if not on the outside, on the inside.

"Emmett Johnson had Hodgkin's disease, and the doctors said he was going to die. But now he's completely cured. It's true that Hodgkin's isn't as serious as what Pastor Karo has, but God does heal."

That didn't seem very comforting right then.

"Why don't we all stand up and hold hands while we pray."

Even though Pastor Swenson was the only one praying out loud, every one of us was praying inside.

That night all of us Salem kids got together and prayed and prayed and prayed. It was hard to believe we all behaved without adult supervision.

In the next few days we really got to know each other, and we really got to know Jesus Christ.

But now, four months later, Pastor is still alive. Anytime now, he could die. But at least he can preach Sunday mornings, after another blood transfusion. It's different now, though. He used to walk all over the platform and wave his arms. Now he has to sit in a chair. No way can he move his arms around. It hurts too much. He needs someone to help him walk. His hands get black and blue if he shakes your hand too hard. Still, he's a great pastor.

But that's leaving out the good part of it all. Because of this disease, I've gotten to know my friends much better. My relationship with God has been growing ever since. And I've really gotten to love Pastor.

This experience has radically changed my life.

9
Christmas Hush

As CHRISTMAS APPROACHED, the thought kept haunting me, *Will this be our last Christmas together?* I wanted to make it the best one ever. I mentioned to Lin one day that we would really have to make this a special Christmas. He did not like that at all. He simply said that this Christmas would be as all others had been. They were always great times, and we would do no more than usual.

A letter helped to make that Christmas special. It was from Janelle Pearson, a woman who had heard Lin's tape-recorded message of "I Believe in God the Father Almighty." She wrote,

> Your message brought me to realize that I had a need in my life. . . . You had just found out about your illness, but you could say, "Lord, I know You are a good and gracious God." I had been in the hospital and when I heard you, I thought, "Wow, that's real faith, that's what I want." That night I put my life in Jesus' hands. . . . Praise God for the miracle He worked in me. First I saw it in you, Nancy, when I could see you smile with the assurance of knowing God is in control, and then I heard it from your witness, Lin, when you said God is in control. . . . I guess that's about all I can tell you right now, except to say that I will always be thankful to God for you

> both. Your lives are testimony of being "born again in Christ."

Letters like that lifted our spirits immeasurably. There was another highly meaningful one from Carol (Mrs. Lee) Eliason.

> It's a little surprising how close we feel to you both in the short time we have been together—but partly I guess it is because you are both so transparent and real that the Lin and Nancy we have gotten to know are really who you are. This makes all the more authentic the sincere faith and trust we have seen in your lives. Maybe you are unaware *how* your real and tested faith in God (as opposed to sentimental, escapist, unrealistic, untried) inspires faith in others—but it does. God being so real to *you* makes Him more real to *us!*

Another unexpected lift came in a check from neighboring Salem Covenant Church. This was the church whose young people had visited our church in November and told Lin they were praying for him. The whole church had joined in the prayer burden. Later children of the church had asked that a portion of the offering at their Christmas program be sent to the local pastor who had cancer. With the check came a message of love and support.

Our Christmas worship service was a moment of holy hush. Lin did not depart from his series on the Apostles' Creed in favor of a more traditional Christmas message. Instead, he pointed out how important was Christ's ascension in the total Christmas story.

* * *

He Ascended into Heaven

The story of Christ's ascension begins in Acts 1:10-11:

> As they were gazing intently into the sky while He was depart-

ing, behold, two men in white clothing stood beside them; and they also said, "Men of Galilee, why do you stand looking into the sky?"

What the angel was really saying is,
"If this Christ has entered into a place of heavenly authority,
then you are not to stand around gazing into heaven.
You get active!"

Colossians 3:1 tells us that Christ is seated
at the right hand of God.
This means that the authority of Christ can now be felt
upon this earth in a new way.
When He walked upon the earth there were only a few
who could enjoy His presence and His healing.
Now *all* of us can.

Jesus, in coming as the Messiah,
came to fulfill three roles.
He came to be a prophet, to be a king,
and to be a priest.
Without the ascension, all three would be void.
That's why the ascension is so important
in understanding the meaning of Christmas.

First, Christ came as a priest
to bring people to a right relationship to God.
He came to bring spiritual healing
to the breach that sin had caused.
However, before the ascension, we must remember
that Christ was limited.
There were only so many people
He was physically able to talk to.
From the human viewpoint, the cross seemed to crush
all possibility of Christ serving as a priest.
The forces of evil seemed to be making a spectacle of Him.
But when Christ arose,

He ascended to His place of authority,
and His priesthood blossomed into new meaning.

Romans 8:34 means a great deal to me right now:

> Who is the one who condemns? Christ Jesus is He who died, yes, rather who was raised, who is at the right hand of God, who also intercedes for us.

Here we see Christ in His *present* priestly role.
Christ can intercede for me and you
because He has entered that heavenly realm
and is not limited by time or space.

On October 27, the day I received the news
that I had taken a definite turn for the worse,
I found it very difficult to pray for healing.
When *you* are ill, I can diligently pray for you.
But when I'm really sick,
I find it very difficult to pray for my own healing.
I feel so unworthy. Why should God heal me?
Look at all the hundreds of others who are not healed.
Why should God do anything special for me?
Especially the way *I* am. I know my own heart.
But a pastor friend reminded me
that God's work does not depend on our worthiness.
We have a High Priest who intercedes for us who believe,
no matter who we are. None of us is worthy of God's favors.
It is interesting that when trouble abounds
and we need to feel accepted, we feel the most unworthy.
But Christ is a High Priest for each of us.
That's why verse 34 means so much to me.
"Who is the one who condemns?"
As I pray for healing, or for anything else,
I know that no one can condemn me
because Christ now has the place of greatest authority.
Christ puts His arms around me as my Priest,
as my Intercessor, and says, "I love you."

You may be bitter,
you may be weighed down with disheartening problems,
but Christ says, "I am your High Priest
and I have *authority* to pray for you."
And that's the difference!
Because of the ascension,
Christ is now in the heavenly realm,
in the place of authority!

I have a team of doctors who are trying to determine
what drugs are the best for me at this time.
These drugs have been tested and found
to retard and kill some tumor-producing cells.
It would be foolish for me to say, "Forget what they say.
I'll ask the man on the street."
We want good doctors
whose authority and judgment we trust.
When we come with our lives to God,
we can know that Christ who intercedes for us
has authority. That's why the ascension is important.

God's sustaining power day by day
is the greatest miracle in my life.
I have a Christ who has authority
and sustains me because He *cares* for me.
My own faith is more deeply confirmed today than ever.
What counts is Christ's overriding power
in the midst of circumstances
that would ordinarily drown us.
He comes to me with peace
on days when it seems impossible.
I am on a great adventure with One who has authority!

Christ is also our King.
Revelation 1:5 says,

> And from Jesus Christ, the faithful witness, the first-born of the dead, and the ruler of the kings of the earth.

Christ is Ruler of kings on earth?
Then why do we have so many bad rulers?
If Christ is the Ruler of all the kings of this earth,
why was there a Hitler?
How can Christ be Ruler of the kings of earth
when we see so much havoc in the world?

Perhaps there is a work going on that we cannot see.
Look at Golgotha. The cross that seemed so cruel
and wrong in history has turned into victory.
In the cross we see how God can take something evil
and make it right the wrongs of mankind.
In the heavenly realm, Christ is working out a tapestry
that I'll understand someday.
I don't like my illness;
I don't like wars or earthquakes.
But at the end of it all,
we will say, "He is King of kings
and Lord of lords, and He has worked out a great plan."

We are also reminded of His kingship by Philippians 2:9-11.
He has been given a name above every name
that every knee should bow before Him.
That helps us understand better what the ascension means.
I may not see every knee bowing before Him now.
We do not see Russia bowing before Him.
We do not even see our materialistic U.S.A.
bowing before Him.
But we must be careful not to make the same mistake
the disciples made during Christ's life.
They wanted a great king.
Their hopes were dashed
as the ministry of Jesus moved irrevocably toward the cross.
They wanted their king to be brought to power.
They wanted the Roman government overthrown.
They wanted Israel lifted up.

And we are like them.
We want the people of God lifted up now.
We want healing now.
We want all the Kingdom to break in upon us now.

God says, "Be patient, people. I'm working a great plan.
The time element will someday
not seem so important to you."

When we first came to the Twin Cities,
Dayton's department store at Christmastime
decorated its windows creatively with animated figures,
and then covered its windows
until a specified day of unveiling.

In a sense, that is what God is doing.
He is working,
but we can't always see what He is doing.
Now and then, He unveils a few things,
but He said, "My *great* creation,
my *new earth,* and my *new* heaven
will someday be revealed to you.
It is being worked on, and you are a part of the process."

The Messiah is also said to be the Prophet.
He was to be the Prophet of all prophets to lead the people,
to bring the fullness of the revelation,
and to give them great gifts.

Ephesians 4:10-11 says,

> He who descended is Himself also He who ascended . . . and He gave some as apostles, and some as prophets, and some as evangelists, and some as pastors and teachers.

The same idea is recorded in the Gospel of John.

> When He, the Spirit of truth, comes, He will guide you into all the truth (16:13).

The work of a prophet is
to bring us the word of truth.
We live in the age of the Spirit
when those gifts are given to the Church
for the upbuilding and guidance of God's people.
The prophetic ministry of Jesus is fulfilled
through the ascension and the coming of the Holy Spirit
upon His Church.

The ascension points to an unlimited Christ.
He is our King, our Priest, our Prophet.
But what does His authority mean in our everyday lives?

The apostle Paul says in Colossians 3:1-4:

> If then you have been raised up with Christ, keep seeking the things above, where Christ is, seated at the right hand of God. Set your mind on the things above, not on the things that are on earth. For you have died and your life is hidden with Christ in God. When Christ, who is our life, is revealed, then you also will be revealed with Him in glory.

What does it mean to seek the things that are above?
Paul tells us in Colossians 3:12-17:

> And so, as those who have been chosen of God, holy and beloved, put on a heart of compassion, kindness, humility, gentleness and patience; bearing with one another, and forgiving each other, whoever has a complaint against any one; just as the Lord forgave you, so also should you. And beyond all these things put on love, which is the perfect bond of unity. And let the peace of Christ rule in your hearts, to which indeed you were called in one body; and be thankful. Let the word of Christ richly dwell within you, with all wisdom teaching and admonishing one another with psalms and hymns and spiritual songs, singing with thankfulness in your hearts to God. And whatever you do in word or deed, do all in the name of the Lord Jesus, giving thanks through Him to God the Father.

Paul is telling us how we, as people of God,
can enjoy the priesthood, the kingship,
the prophetic ministry,
and get involved with one another.

We don't experience it in isolation.
The relationship of Christians with each other
is the greatest gift I have experienced in my sickness.
We are the people of God.
The ascended Christ has given us to each other.
He says we are to enjoy one another,
love one another,
be kind to one another.
In so doing, we will experience
the ascended Christ in our midst.

On this Christmas Eve
I feel that God is doing a work in your hearts
and in mine.
He has drawn us very close to each other,
and I believe this is the greatest gift to our church.
I think we have experienced a great renewal,
a great outpouring of God's love.
May it continue to be so.

* * *

We were alone for Christmas Eve, and we felt added closeness as a family. The excitement of the kids, the wonderment of our three-year-old, and the deep meaning of Christmas made this a very special time.

On Tuesday Lin began a persistent cough, and he eventually began coughing blood. He had another disappointing surprise that day. He looked in the mirror and noticed that his face was getting round. He had already noticed that his feet and legs were swelling and he knew it was reaction to the Prednisone, another of the drugs he was taking.

When we went to the clinic on Wednesday for his regular appointment, the doctors decided to readmit him to try to find the cause for the abdominal pain he was now experiencing as well as the coughing of blood.

With Lin admitted again, I turned for help to the Scriptures, and that night I had an unusual experience. I felt I was beginning to see what James meant when he said, "Count it all joy, my brethren, when you encounter various trials" (1:2). I had experienced joy after previous trials; now there was joy during this particular trial. I waited to see what God was doing.

Not finding anything any more abnormal than before, the doctors discharged Lin two days later, on December 29, and told him to continue treatment in the clinic.

On Sunday, December 31, Lin spoke on "He Shall Come to Judge."

* * *

He Shall Come to Judge

In Matthew 24:36-44 we have some of the teaching of Jesus
about judgment.
In this passage, He warned His hearers
that there is a style of life
that will separate them from God.

> But of that day and hour no one knows, not even the angels of heaven, nor the Son, but the Father alone. For the coming of the Son of Man will be just like the days of Noah. For as in those days which were before the flood they were eating and drinking, they were marrying and giving in marriage, until the day that NOAH ENTERED THE ARK, and they did not understand until the flood came and took them all away, so shall the coming of the Son of Man be. Then there shall be two men in the field; one will be taken, and one will be left. Two women will be grinding at the mill; one will be taken, and one will be left. Therefore be on the alert, for you do not know which day your Lord is coming. But be sure of this, that if the

head of the house had known at what time of the night the thief was coming, he would have been on the alert and would not have allowed his house to be broken into. For this reason you be ready too; for the Son of Man is coming at an hour when you do not think He will.

This portion of Scripture shows us
that Christ comes to judge our *false* securities.
We all have certain things that we count secure.
Verse 38 describes some people this way:
"They were eating and drinking,
marrying and giving in marriage."
What's so wrong about that?
We all eat and drink and most of us marry.

In these things
the people were finding a false sense of *immortality*.
Everything was going to keep on going as it was.
Nothing was going to change.
And that kind of security
may give us a "god complex."
We feel we have things under control
and can pretty much chart our lives
in whatever direction we choose.

One day in the middle of August
changed my whole direction of life.
On that day I was told I had cancer.
Before that I thought I was living my life
really dependent on God
and that I didn't have false securities.
I was wrong.
I was assuming that everything was going to go on
as it was.
If someone was going to get cancer,
it would be the other guy, not me.
If anyone was going to die shortly,
it would be someone else, not me.

We all play that game, don't we?
Someday we will each face death.
Until that time, we cling to the idea
that everything is going to carry on just as it is.
That's why death is such a shock to us.
It reminds us of our finitude.

But isn't this really a judgment
that reminds us of our humanity?
Most of us would like to argue with God about death.
But no matter how we argue or ignore the subject,
it is there for everyone. We cannot avoid it.
The people in the days of Noah
thought everything would go on as usual.
They would eat, drink, marry,
give in marriage, just as always.
But God brought His judgment.

What is your style of life?
You eat in the morning, at noon, and at night;
you go to work, come home,
go to bed, get up in the morning,
and start the whole routine over again.

Where is God?
Where was God in the lives of the people of Noah's day?

The man who thinks everything is going to continue
as it is has a second false security.
He is ignorant of God.
Our life-styles indicate whether we are ignorant of God.
How important is He to our daily lives?
To our goals in life?
To our priorities?
The people of Noah's day ignored God
in their life-style, and God judged them.

If we are just eating, drinking,
marrying, giving in marriage,
and ignoring God, we are useless.

We also need to remember that the judgment of God is *now.*
In Romans 1:16-18 we usually notice only verse 16.
But I want us to look especially at verses 17 and 18. Verse 16 reads,

> For I am not ashamed of the gospel, for it is the power of God for salvation to every one who believes, to the Jew first and also to the Greek.

Then in verses 17 and 18, Paul writes,

> For in it the righteousness of God is revealed from faith to faith; as it is written, BUT THE RIGHTEOUS MAN SHALL LIVE BY FAITH." For the wrath of God is revealed from heaven against all ungodliness and unrighteousness of men, who suppress the truth in unrighteousness.

I want to give you a very literal translation of verse 17.
It says "the righteousness of God is *being* revealed."
Actually, God's righteousness *is now being* revealed
through God's people.
God's way of making men righteous
is being revealed today through His Church.
Verse 18 shows the other side:
"The *wrath* of God is also *being* revealed from heaven
against all ungodliness and unrighteousness of men."
Just as God's way of making men right with Himself
is being revealed, so the judgment of God
is also being revealed in men's lives.

How is the judgment of God being revealed in our lives?
I want to share with you a poem
that was sent to me by a young lady
who came to faith in Christ through hearing the tape
of the first sermon I had on the Apostles' Creed.

She tells what life was like
for her *before* she became a Christian.

I have my family,
I have my health,
I have some joy,
I have some wealth.
And still there is a void.

I have friends,
I have a home.
I have freedom,
Room to roam,
And still there is a void.

I have almost all the world can give.
I have enough to get me by.
And yet, I still am sad.
I feel like I could cry.
Because there's still a void.

If you are going your own way, independent of God,
you have a void.
That is the judgment of God upon your life.
If you are a Christian, you may still be walking
contrary to what God wants for you
and missing the relationship that you should have
with God. God is judging our lives.

But there is also a positive side to this.
John 5:24 reads,

> Truly, truly, I say to you, he who hears My word, and believes Him who sent Me, has eternal life, and does not come into judgment, but has passed out of death into life.

The word "judgment" would be clearer here if it were
translated "condemnation":

> He does not come into *condemnation,* but is passed out of death into life.

Some have quoted this verse to try to teach

that Christians shall never be judged.
That is wrong.
We will all stand before God
and give account of ourselves.
But the believer will not be condemned.

The man who does not know Christ
will be judged for his life-style,
and also will be condemned for not trusting in Christ.
If our life-style is placed under the lordship of Christ,
we have nothing to fear.
In fact, we are rewarded.
But in those areas where our lives are still self-centered,
we experience the judgment of God.
We must understand that we will not
come into condemnation,
but we are all standing *now* before God being judged.

The way God is judging your life right now affects your future.
If you have discovered the liberation that Christ gives,
you are now free to live
under the lordship of Jesus Christ.
Then, in the future, you will not know condemnation.

Look again at John 5:24:

> He who hears My word, and believes Him who sent Me, has eternal life.

We often think of eternal life as duration of time,
as a life that goes on forever.
If so, we have missed the real meaning of eternal life.
Eternal life refers to a quality of life.
Every person is caught and imprisoned
by his own self-centeredness.
We cannot deliver ourselves.
But when we hear the Word of God
and trust Christ as our Saviour,
a miracle happens—the miracle of liberation.

We are now freed from our self-centered prison
so we can be open to people and to seeing them as persons.
Only then can we begin to understand
what is called the Kingdom of God, or the rule of God.

The rule of God is made up of four right relationships.
First, I have a right relationship with God.
Whereas I once considered myself independent from God,
I now totally depend upon Him.
He is my Friend and my Saviour,
my Guide through life.
I have known the forgiveness of sins through Jesus Christ.

Second, I have a right relationship with myself;
I have been liberated.
I am no longer a self-centered person;
rather, I now live in *dependence* upon God.
I know what it is to be liberated
and to be able to appreciate myself for the way God made me.
This happens because my relationship with God
has been straightened out.

Third, I have a right relationship
with the other significant people in my life.
The others who are significant are the members of my family
and the people of my church,
the family of God.
I appreciate them and I realize I'm a part of a family,
and that we help one another.

Fourth, I have a right relationship to the world.
I now see the world as people in need,
and I'm concerned about them.
And that is the rule of God in this world.

Jesus said He came to bring the Kingdom of God,
the rule of God.

It has not yet come in all its fullness.
If the Kingdom of God had come in all its fullness,
I would be able to stand up to preach.
I wouldn't have this cancer gnawing at me.
The Kingdom has not come in its fullness,
but it has come in these right relationships.

Every person who trusts Christ as his Saviour
is on the road to right relationships with God,
with himself,
with others who are significant,
and with the world.
Those are beautiful relationships,
but each of them must grow.
If we grow only in one area,
we create a kind of monster,
but when we grow in all four relationships,
the development is beautiful.

Why don't we grow as we ought?
Because the devil sometimes gets us turned back
on ourselves.
Christ liberates us,
but we may get so concerned about ourselves
and our organizations that we forget
we are liberated people!
If we have these right relationships,
we need to share them with the world.
If we don't, we soon become joyless.
But when our lives show these right relationships,
there is an impact!

The judgment of God also means that
ultimately God will be victorious.
If you were in my shoes this morning,
you would know why this is so important.

You see, God not only judges *sin,*
but He also judges the *results* of sin.
That means cancer and all other kinds of illness.
One day I won't have to worry about cancer
because God will judge it.
Furthermore, there is a day coming
when God will gather us all together.

My favorite hymn has become "For All the Saints."
It expresses the glory of that day
when He will gather together *all* His saints.
I look forward to that day
when He will have judged *all* disease
and *all* sin, and we shall
be gathered as His people.
Like everything else about our great God,
His judgment is good.
We can rejoice that He is coming
to judge the quick and the dead.

10

A New Year of Hope

DURING THE AFTERNOON of December 31, Lin's cough kept getting worse, and he began to feel as though he might have the flu. By the next morning, he was worse. Steve, Rob, and Scotty had all been sick with what seemed like the flu. I was so physically weary of running up and down steps to care for all of them that I wondered how long I could go on. When I crawled into bed that evening, I had a silent cry. (I felt I could not let Lin hear me.) And I prayed. I seemed to visualize Christ's actual presence; and it was as though I was crying on His shoulder, and He was saying, "Cast all your care upon Me, for I care for you!" Then I was able to relax and sleep.

The next day Lin was scheduled to go to the clinic. His intern, Dave Opsahl, had arranged for him to go directly to his usual room in 7 South to have blood drawn and to be checked over instead of waiting in the clinic. When the results came back, Lin asked Dave how the counts were and Dave did not respond. Finally he said, "Pretty bad. You'll have to stay here. There may be the possibility of pneumonia."

My heart sank.

They immediately began intravenous solutions of antibiotics, and I went home. That night I read in the Bible,

"I have been very thoroughly initiated into the human lot with all its ups and downs. . . . I have strength for anything through him who gives me power. But it was kind of you to share the burden of my troubles" (Philippians 4:12-14, NEB).

I knew I could lean on God, His power, and His people.

The next day we asked Dave to tell us what the white count had actually been the day before. It had been 137,000. (The normal is between 5,000 and 10,000.) Furthermore, there was 85 percent of malignant cells.

The same day, I had a phone call saying that my dad had a heart attack and was now hospitalized in California. That news turned Lin's concern from himself to my father, for they were very close; but he was still very alert to his own situation. During the evening, when the nurse brought his Methotrexate pills, he noticed that there seemed to be more than usual. He questioned the nurse about it, but she assured him that it was the correct dosage.

Later on the nurse realized she *had* given him the wrong dosage, and she recorded the actual number of tablets given. However, she did not report her error to the doctors.

The next day, when routine white-blood counts were done, it was discovered that his had dropped dramatically from 137,000 to 5,000!

Checking back over the records, the doctors found that he had been given twice as much Methotrexate as had been ordered. In the providence of God, the error turned out to bring good results, although in other circumstances it could have been disastrous. At any rate, the doctors were overjoyed at the results of the error and felt that his body might be supersensitive to this dosage of Methotrexate and this sensitivity could be used successfully to combat the cancer.

For the first time in months, the doctors felt they had a drug combination (using Methotrexate and one called 6-

Thioguanine) that could bring a long-term remission and control of the cancer.

On January 4, Lin's mother came again from California to visit and to help out. Lin needed her and so did I. I met her at the airport and took her directly to the hospital to see Lin. We arrived just as the doctors were telling Lin the good news about the possible remission.

We were all overjoyed. Every day for the next week the medical reports were consistently encouraging.

By January 7, the white-cell count had dropped to 3,000 and there was only 10 percent of malignant cells showing in the blood smear.

Everything was good about that day. When I arrived home, the women from the church had been there again to give the house a good cleaning. I took Robby to his first hockey game of the season, and his team won, 2 to 1.

Two days later, on January 9, there was only 3 percent of malignant cells. The next day, when the doctors arrived with their report, Emmett Johnson, of the Minnesota Baptist Conference, was visiting. We waited breathlessly. The doctors reported there were *no* malignant cells showing in the blood. Emmett ran for the phone to share the news with others at conference headquarters. Lin broke out in a cold sweat all over. We were a jubilant group that afternoon. The doctors did add, however, that they were scheduling a bone-marrow test to determine exactly what was happening in the blood.

We were so happy we felt nothing could bring discouragement.

That evening a flu epidemic hit the hospital wing where Lin was a patient, and 7 South was put in isolation. That meant no visitors.

Later, as Lin's mother and I were eating supper at home, she complained of pains in the abdomen. They rapidly became severe, so I rushed her to Unity Hospital near our home. She had had similar pain a few years earlier that proved to be a bowel obstruction that required surgery. She feared a repeat episode. She was sedated and underwent a battery of tests. Nothing was positive. But I had to call Lin and tell him that his mother was now in another hospital twenty-five miles away from him but that the doctors did not think it was anything serious. I again began to feel as though I were drowning in responsibilities.

Shortly afterward, one of the members of Salem, Clifford Anderson, tried to see Lin, but was kept out because of the flu isolation of Lin's section. So instead of visiting Lin, he phoned him from the hall. Lin told Cliff of his mother's problem and asked him to go to Unity Hospital and see if any assistance was needed. He arrived just when I needed him! Because Lin's mother had been heavily sedated, she had trouble walking. Cliff helped me get her into the car as we returned from the hospital, and he followed us home, helping me get her into the house. The next day she was much better.

With his new encouragement for the future, Lin wrote a letter to the pastors of the Minnesota Conference. He was still realistic about his disease.

> DEAR FELLOW PASTORS:
>
> "So do not be anxious about tomorrow; tomorrow will look after itself, Each day has troubles enough of its own."*
>
> One of the great lessons of life is learning to live a day at a time. I am desperately trying to learn this lesson.
>
> In August I entered the hospital discovering I had a form of cancer called lymphosarcoma. There was a very large tumor in the middle of the chest. I started chemical treat-

*Matthew 6:34 (NEB)

ment and the tumor seemed to disappear after two series of treatments. There was great hope. I returned to my church with new enthusiasm. I had wondered in August if I would ever enter the pulpit again, but by September God had given me new life to preach. Preaching took on new excitement for me because God was becoming so important day by day. I was going through a new discovery of Him. Then in October I became very ill again and we found the disease had taken some very bad turns. Now I am told that there is no cure and that it is a matter of time before the disease will run its course and end my life. This may be a long period, perhaps a year or more.

But God has sustained me during this time in a very special way. I am not a courageous person. But I have discovered that God gives His peace for every circumstance. That is a miracle. Peace means wholeness and if someone a year ago told me I could know peace in the midst of these problems I would have thought "impossible." But I have discovered that peace for each day. In fact, life has taken on a whole new dimension of adventure with God. What a great discovery to find that when everything falls out from under you, there is *God.* The really amazing thing is the fact that the harder circumstances get, the greater God gets.

Preaching also has taken on new excitement even though I must sit and preach because I do not have enough strength to stand.

As I look at where I now am in my adventure with God, I ask that you pray with me that God will intervene and destroy this evil disease through the discovery of a new miracle drug or by supernatural intervention. I appreciate the concern and prayers of so many of you.

What a great privilege we have as pastors to relate to the people of God the message of God as it really is. I live for each Sunday to be with the people of God. The amazing

> thing is that I think they look forward to each Sunday. It is a great adventure. Whether you suffer or are in good health, we all have the peace of God for everything. Keep up the good work, men of God; there will be a day when we will work no more!

On January 11, a spinal tap was done; no cells were found in it, nor were there any malignant cells in the blood. A bone-marrow test was scheduled for the next morning. That night we prayed fervently that the bone marrow would show that good cells were now being produced instead of malignant cells.

The bone-marrow test was a disappointment. It showed that malignant cells were still present, but healthy ones seemed to predominate. However, the flu that had hit the hospital seemed to be hitting Lin now. He was running a fever and feeling generally bad. The isolation ban was lifted on January 12, and we were again allowed to visit Lin. His mother was feeling fine by now so she was able to spend the day with him. He still wasn't feeling well, but it seemed more like a cold than the flu and they were again giving antibiotics.

As often seemed to happen, God sent His ministering angels when Lin needed them the most. One came in the form of a letter from Art Rouner, pastor of Colonial church in Edina, who had often come to visit Lin.

> DEAR LIN, MY BEAUTIFUL BROTHER:
>
> How great to see you Tuesday. You are God's special man. He touches me so deeply through you. I have such trouble getting to a book of theology or a book of great sermons and there you are, flat on your back in the hospital with Helmut Thielicke right at your side!
>
> So, you see, I learn from you, too. Maybe I'll be a better scholar and surely a more faithful preacher by standing

next to a man who in the best classic sense, speaks with Richard Baxter, seventeenth century Puritan, "as dying man to dying men."

Which is not in any way to say something ominous about your future. I am so heartened and encouraged by the great news you shared with me yesterday. I'm believing you have more time ahead of you than even the doctors suspect or hope for in their wildest imaginings. We are counting on life for you and a long and powerful and growing ministry.

But the authentic note. That's the gift so hard to come by in modern preaching. The note of authority. The voice of one who speaks almost from the other side. One who can say, "I stood in the dark and I saw the light." Who can say, "I, too, am a sinful man, and I have been saved." Who can say, "I hurt, as so many of you have hurt and One came to me and touched me and gave me life." The power of Jesus is that He went all the way. God went to the Cross in Him and took it all for us and, in a real sense, you are taking it all for your people, hanging there in pain for them. Standing in the gap for them. And so powerfully and beautifully calling across the miles of experience to them, saying, "It's all right. There's hope. God is real. Jesus is Lord. Mine and yours!" You are an open channel for God's Holy Spirit and how exciting to see Him work in you.

As my Pentecostal buddies say, "Praise the Lord!" In fact, "Hallelujah!"

Love you, dear friend. Bless you. Love to your family and to all your people.

Your friend in the greatest cause,

ARTHUR A. ROUNER, JR.

Early Tuesday, January 16, Lin's mother went to the hospital with Dr. Carl Christenson to visit with Lin until she had to leave for California at noon. She found him clearly worse. He was extremely tired, which we assumed was caused by the congestion of the cold. His hemoglobin was very low, and his white-cell count had dropped to 400. He was too sick to visit with her. At noon I took her to the airport.

Shortly after she left at noon, further reports came on his bone marrow. It showed that the marrow was producing healthy cells! Lin's spirits perked up, especially when he was told he could go home the next day. He was given four pints of blood so he would feel better.

As soon as he began to feel better, his mind reverted back to his great love, preaching, and how much he wanted to serve the church this way. Lee Eliason visited him and they again discussed this calling and need which Lin felt so keenly.

"We talked about his sense of the need for great evangelical preachers," Lee said. "He had a dream of great preaching that was very stimulating to me. He felt a preacher should be very biblical, not necessarily using Bible phrases all the time, but communicating the truth of God in the language of the people today. He asked me, 'Who's going to do it, Lee?' He wanted to be a great preacher, not for ego's sake, but because of what happens in people's lives when someone preaches God's truth well."

Lin came home on Wednesday, January 17, but by evening he was feeling nauseated. His temperature went up that night, but dropped again in the morning. Every evening, the same cycle repeated. On Saturday evening, January 20, when his temperature reached 104 degrees, I called Dr. Taddeini, and he said, "Come to the hospital at once."

Lin's reply to me was "I'm almost getting tired of fighting this." That surprised me, because his desire to fight the disease was so all-consuming. We both felt depressed. We had been so sure he would be out of the hospital for a good long time. After all, hadn't the tests been encouraging for the first time in weeks?

After I said good-bye to him (a friend from church took him back to the hospital so I could stay with our boys), I felt deeply discouraged. I read Psalm 21, and verse 4 stood out from the others: "He asked life of Thee, Thou didst give it to him, length of days forever and ever." It encouraged me. Perhaps God was saying that I would have Lin with me for some time yet.

Everything went wrong on that trip back to the hospital. He could not get into his usual room or wing because it was overcrowded, so he was placed in a wing where the staff knew little about him. He had interminable waits for a bed to be made, for a wheelchair to get to his room, etc.; and when he arrived, a new intern insisted on doing a complete series of admitting procedures and examinations. He was desperately ill, running a high fever, and he was kept awake for examinations until 3 A.M.!

When he called the next morning and told me the ordeal he had gone through in being admitted, I sank to a new low.

I went to church as usual. When Lee asked how Lin was doing, I was able to relate what had happened. But when he asked how *I* was doing, I broke into tears. The whole service was a weepy time for me. Lee's message was, appropriately, "How God Sustains Us." I felt he was speaking to me directly when he said, "The point is, when the chips are down, where is God?" The chips were surely down for us. God had been with us and He would continue to be with us. It was a reminder I needed, as did others in the Salem family.

On Sunday night, Lin and I did a foolish thing, both of us separately and unwittingly. One of the local TV stations was doing a series on death, and this Sunday night followed a case history of a young man with cancer—and wouldn't you know it—it was lymphosarcoma, the same rare disease that Lin had. Of course, after the program began I could not turn it off. I watched as the young man went through remissions, hospitalizations, and finally death, about one year after the cancer was discovered. It was a terrible night. I reread Psalms 20 and 21.

The next day I learned that Lin had watched it, too, and had gone through his own soul struggle at the hospital. It made both of us turn more and more to the sustaining power of God. Even through these discouraging times, the strength and comfort of God were upholding Lin. He did not complain about what was happening to him. About this time, he said to Steve one evening, "Never look back, Steve."

By Tuesday, just three days after admittance, the doctors were back with more encouraging news. They said they now considered him a "retrievable" patient and were thinking in terms of years rather than months.

It was like a new lease on life for Lin. He figured this would buy time, giving medical science more time to find that cure for cancer. And always, Lin knew, God could step in and bring about a miraculous healing. Lin so much wanted a cure for cancer, not only for himself, but for the many other patients he was meeting. This became a constant prayer for him and for me.

About a week later, on Sunday, January 28, my parents arrived from San Jose, California. Dad had just been released from the hospital following his heart attack, and the doctors felt it would be good for him to get back here and spend some time with Lin, for they felt that his problem had been due in part to his concern for Lin.

The next day, on January 29, Lin was released from the

hospital. It was the seventh time we made the trip home, and it was the best one ever. For the last few days he had been able to get along without the eye patch. On the way home in the car he exulted over being able to read the signs and to see one car at a time instead of everything in double. He was jubilant and so were the doctors. The rest of the week he rested and worked on his next sermons, and on February 4 he was back in the pulpit for the first time in more than a month.

His clothes hung loosely on his gaunt frame, his face was very pale, and he knew he would have to sit to preach, but he was so thrilled to be there.

When he walked in, he was astonished to see that the church was packed with 425 people. Children were even sitting on the floor of the unfinished balcony.

As Lee Eliason stood to lead the service he said, "As is the custom at Salem when something special happens, we want to express our thanks to God for bringing Pastor Karo back to us." The people began applauding and the applause went on and on for several minutes. Sitting in the front row of the choir, I tried to hold back the tears, but I could not. Many of the people in the congregation were weeping with me.

Lin sat down at his "preaching table" and spoke on "I Believe in the Holy Ghost."

* * *

I Believe in the Holy Ghost

It's great to be back with you again after four weeks.
  I kept hoping each Sunday that I'd be here.
  This Sunday I was determined to make it
    even though I have had a bad week.

The medicines seemed to make me sleep
about twenty-two hours
out of every twenty-four.
I prayed that somehow God would give me strength
to prepare this message.
Hopefully, we have some good things going
for us medically now,
and I believe that God is doing some great things.

I have often introduced you to my doctors who have come
to visit. Today, one of the nurses is in the congregation.
Pat Edwards. She has been very kind
and patient with me.

In John 3:1-8 we read,

> Now there was a man of the Pharisees, named Nicodemus, a ruler of the Jews; this man came to Him [Jesus] by night, and said to Him, "Rabbi, we know that You have come from God as a teacher; for no one can do these signs that you do unless God is with him." Jesus answered and said to him, "Truly, truly, I say to you, unless one is born again, he cannot see the kingdom of God." Nicodemus said to Him, "How can a man be born when he is old? He cannot enter a second time into his mother's womb and be born, can he?" Jesus answered, "Truly, truly I say to you, unless one is born of water and the Spirit, he cannot enter into the kingdom of God. That which is born of the flesh is flesh; and that which is born of the Spirit is spirit. Do not marvel that I said to you, 'You must be born again.' The wind blows where it wishes and you hear the sound of it, but do not know where it comes from and where it is going; so is every one who is born of the Spirit."

We say we believe in the Holy Spirit. But if we are pressed
as to *what* we believe about the Holy Spirit
and what we have *experienced* of the Holy Spirit,
we become a bit anxious.
There is a mystery about the Holy Spirit.

Jesus uses the wind as His figure of speech.
Actually, wind and spirit are the same word
in the language Jesus used.
Jesus carefully chose this word
and figure of speech because the wind *is* mysterious.
Sometimes on a warm summer evening
a breeze is refreshingly welcome.
But on other nights when the sky is threatening,
and the wind turns to a gale,
I am afraid. Winds are mysterious.

The mystery about the Holy Spirit may cause us to pull back.
Perhaps the subject of the Holy Spirit
is one you would like to shelve for awhile.
Let's take it off the shelf and try to see what God intended.
The Holy Spirit is here among us
to help us carry on our work as witnesses.

Nicodemus, before his talk with Jesus,
knew nothing of the Holy Spirit.
Yet Nicodemus was extremely religious.
Nicodemus, like other Pharisees, was troubled by Jesus.
Jesus was not fitting into the picture
they had outlined for the Messiah.
But Nicodemus was the only one who had the gumption
to go to Jesus to hear what He had to say.
Nicodemus said to Jesus,
"You must be a great teacher sent from God
because You have done some terrific things
and You have the whole town excited."

Jesus answered, "Nicodemus, you must be born again
if you are going to see the Kingdom of God."
Being "born again"
has become a popular phrase to us.

We tell people, "You have to be born again
if you are to see the Kingdom of God."

But do *we* understand what experience Jesus was saying
that Nicodemus must have?
Nicodemus already had a good religion,
and he was practicing it the best he could.

But Jesus was saying, "Nicodemus, the rule of God
is coming upon us in great force,
but you'll miss it all
if you are not born by the Holy Spirit."

He was saying, "Something must happen, Nicodemus,
that brings about a new quality of life
that you cannot provide for yourself.
It can be provided only by the Holy Spirit.
Only He can take you out of your prison of self-centeredness."

I remember when I was born of the Spirit.
Late one night as I lay in bed,
I began thinking about something a lady had told me.
She said I needed Christ as my Saviour.
I was fifteen years old and I had heard it before.
But that night it clicked.
I got down on my knees and said,
"I don't understand everything about this,
but one thing I do understand is that I am a sinner
and I need the Saviour, Jesus Christ."

Jesus used the wind to teach Nicodemus certain lessons.
For some of my ideas on verse 8,
I am indebted to the great preacher, James Stewart.
Verse 8 starts with, "The wind blows."
In this figure of speech about the wind,
I think Jesus was saying,
"Nicodemus, the Holy Spirit is like the wind.
It is always at work."

There are different kinds of winds.

Occasionally the wind is a refreshing breeze.
We like to be in places where the Holy Spirit
moves like a refreshing breeze among God's people.
The Holy Spirit comes not only on one individual
to make him stand out, but more often to make a harmony,
an orchestra, from His people.
He comes upon His *people* and gives them certain gifts
to do His work in His *community*.

But there are times when the Holy Spirit
does not come like a refreshing breeze,
but instead like a roaring tornado.
He seems to tear God's people apart,
perhaps because we are so deeply rooted in our routine
or in our religion
or in our hypocrisy,
that it takes a tornado to lift us out
of that kind of life-style.

I feel as if I have been torn apart in the last six months
by the Holy Spirit.
It has been a great adventure with God.
The Holy Spirit has done wonderful things in my life,
and I know that He has done wonderful things
in some of your lives.
But it has not been a gentle breeze.
At times I wondered if we were going to weather the storm.
But like the wind that sometimes blows gently,
and sometimes furiously,
the Holy Spirit is at work among His people.

In Acts 2, the coming of the Holy Spirit is described
as a mighty wind coming upon the people.
Do you sense that in your own life?
Or are you still sitting on the fringe
wondering what *is* going on?

I trust that the wind is blowing in your life
and that you are having an experience with the Holy Spirit.

When Jesus says, "The wind blows where it wishes,"
He is talking about the sovereignty of the Holy Spirit.
When we lived in southern California, we looked forward
to the Santa Ana winds each fall.
They were hot but they blew the smog out over the ocean
and made the days clear.
Scientists have never been able to figure out
how to control those Santa Ana winds
and thus control the smog.

Jesus said, "The wind blows where it wishes.
You can't do a thing about it, Nicodemus."
That's how the Spirit is.
We would like to control the Holy Spirit
so that we could predict what He will do.
I used to think "the wind blows where it wishes"
meant that if the Holy Spirit does not want
to come into my life, He won't come.
That is not what it means.

In fact, I found a new and positive application
in my own experience this past week.
I found myself not much on fire for the Lord.
Now, you'd think that with everything I've gone through
and as good as God has been to me,
I'd be singing hallelujah all the time.
Well, I'm not.
Last week when I found myself at a low point,
the truth of this portion hit me.
It said that even though my heart is hard,
and I don't feel worthy of the Holy Spirit,
He still comes into my life.
I am still a child of His.
He still gets through to me.

You may be feeling extremely low, thinking,
"How can God accept me?"
The Holy Spirit says, "I'll come into your life
because I will come where I will.
Although you feel unworthy and unaccepted,
here I come."
The Holy Spirit is sovereign.
Be careful that you don't try to control the Holy Spirit,
or design Him,
but rather seek to discover Him.
Life then becomes an adventure because He has many
surprises for you.

In Acts 2, we see a demonstration of the Holy Spirit.
The observers at the day of Pentecost
knew something had happened
because those believers were now different.
The people who had gathered in the upper room
had been scaredy-cats.
They were afraid to speak out for the Lord.

After the Holy Spirit came upon them,
they were bold. Look at Peter's sermon.
I've analyzed that sermon, and there's nothing great
about it that I can see.
Instead, he reviews the most recent history of the town
and the gossip of the day that the people already knew.
But he says, "It is not gossip. It is truth."
And something seemed to click with the people.
That something was the Holy Spirit coming into their lives.
These people, who before were hiding from others,
were now speaking boldly.

How do we know that the Holy Spirit is at work among us?
It must show in the quality of life we live.
It's what Jesus meant by the new kind of life.

It is new awareness of the rule of God in this world.
We are on an adventure with God.

I don't know what the Holy Spirit has for us.
We have heard the wind blowing.
Where is He taking us?
When is He coming again afresh upon us
as the people of God?
I have prayed that it would be this morning.
Do you feel that the Holy Spirit is speaking to you,
pointing to the kind of life-style that God intended for you?
Do you feel your need for the wind of the Spirit
to come again over your life?

I'm not talking about a second blessing,
but rather of your sense
that you *really* are committed to God.
I'm still trying to work out what it really means
to be committed to God,
what it really means for the Holy Spirit
to bring about this new quality of life.

What is the quality of life for the one born
into the family of God?
You begin to ask yourself those questions
when you face life and death and all of its realities.
Is the wind of the Spirit blowing through your life
and demonstrating His presence?

It isn't enough to "believe" in the Holy Spirit.
We must also experience His work in our lives.

* * *

Lin even felt well enough to lead the evening service which included the Lord's Supper that day. He spoke briefly about John the Baptist and his confused faith as to whether Jesus was the Messiah (see Matthew 11:3-6). Attendance was so large that the church ran out of Communion cups for the service. A spirit of oneness and praise to God dominated the evening.

11

Courage to Fight On

On Tuesday, Lin wanted very much to attend the annual Founders' Week meetings at Bethel College and Seminary, just a five-minute drive from our home. The main speaker was to be Roger Fredrikson, pastor of First Baptist Church of Sioux Falls, South Dakota. His ministry had meant a lot to Lin while he was in seminary when Fredrikson had come several times as a guest speaker.

Dad and I agreed to take Lin on one condition—that he go in a wheelchair. He balked at that, insisting that he felt better and had sufficient strength in his legs. But we were adamant. Lin later admitted that he could never have walked the distance from the entryway.

Fredrikson saw Lin there, and when he finished his sermon he told the audience about Lin and his battle with cancer. He asked that people who were seated near Lin go over and place their hands gently on him. Then he led the vast congregation in prayer for Lin's healing. It was a great experience of sensing God's people reaching out and caring.

That afternoon, Fredrikson came over and visited with Lin. They shared experiences in the Word, and Lin shared his adventure with cancer and God's care and provision during this difficult time.

Now Lin began working eagerly on his next sermons. The excitement of preaching again pushed him on, even though he found it a struggle to study. He felt that he was not able to prepare as he would have liked, and he seemed to sense that he was growing weaker rather than stronger. But he and my dad sat by the hour discussing topic after topic, both convalescing, both eager to grow in understanding of God and His Word.

On February 18, Lin's face was more drawn; his clothes hung more loosely, but his voice seemed to have the same old power. He told the people that at the close of the service he would sit at the table in front—as he had done previously—to greet them, but that he would not be able to shake their hands. His blood platelet count had become so low that he got severe bruises even from a handshake. The congregation sang his favorite hymn, "For All the Saints" and he preached on "I Believe in the Holy Catholic Church."

* * *

I Believe in the Holy Catholic Church

Everyone today is talking about what is wrong with the Church,
and there is a lot we can talk about:
the apathy,
the traditionalism,
the seemingly program-oriented,
attendance-oriented,
impersonal attitude of many Church people.
We all have great diagnostic skills;
what we are looking for are cures.
It is something like my illness.
The doctors know exactly what kind of cancer I have,
but they don't really know how to cure me.
However, every suggested and possible treatment
rests on some understanding of my body and how it works.

Today we are discussing "The Holy Catholic Church,"
what it is and how it works.
First let's look at the word "Holy."
It is one of those words we jump back from.
But we should note that "Holy" actually means "different, separated unto someone else."
The Church is meant to be different from the world,
a community separated unto God.
That separation is not to be detachment from the world.
Rather, it is separated in the sense
that it points beyond itself.
This was a new concept to the ancient world.
The Church was to include all—Gentile, Jew, slave,
free, Greek, barbarian, man, woman.
God's Church must by its very nature be universal.

The word "Catholic" simply means "whole" or "universal."
The whole Church does not mean
only the people of God at Salem Baptist.
There are millions outside of our confined walls
who are part of the Church.
We can find them in every nation
and in every city.
The Church is a gathered community
given over to the guidance of God
under the lordship of Jesus Christ.

These days the Church is criticized for its programs,
its buildings,
its tradition.
Perhaps some of this criticism is justified.
How do we measure success?
By the numbers of people who attend?
By the size of the budget?
By whether this year's program
outdoes last year's program?
The Church is not numbers and budgets and programs.

If it is not these things, what is the Church?
First, the Church is people.
We speak so often of a building as the Church
that we tend to forget that the Church is *people.*
The structure witnesses to the community
that a Church gathers *inside* the building.
A good building may *help* us serve people,
but we must never forget that serving people in all places
is our real purpose.

The people who make up the Church are given certain names
in the Bible, and these names
help us understand the Church.
The Church is made up of Christians.
The word *Christian* started in Antioch as a nickname.
It started as a derogatory label.
But today it has become a name of honor.
We are Christ folk, or Christ followers.

The second name given to the people of God,
the Church, was "saint."
A saint is one who is different from the world
and is separated unto God.
Are you a saint?
Most of us recoil from that word and say,
"There are only a few people who fit that category,
and I am not one of them."
But every believer *is* a saint.
You are a saint, for you are called out from the world
and separated unto God for His special use.

Another name given Christians is "disciple,"
which means learner.
When you hear the term "disciple"
you think immediately of Christ's twelve disciples.
But a Christ follower, a Christian,
is also a disciple when he is a learner.

Another name is "believer."
"Believer" means that a person has faith in certain truths
and acts on them.
We are committed to Christ and His truths.

The word "servant" is used.
This shows the absolute authority of Christ over our lives.
We get the meaning of this term from the Old Testament.
The master had authority over the servant.

Another more intimate term is "brother."
This emphasizes that our new relationship with God
brings a new relationship with one another.

Having been in the hospital for a month,
there are many of you who are new
and whose names I don't know.
This is embarrassing to me
because you *are* my brothers and sisters.
Apparently some things that were important
to the early Church
have become less important to us.
We would rather know how many we had in Sunday school
than if someone met a new brother or sister in Christ today.
Do we come home and say,
"Man, we set a new record today"?
Or, "Man, I met a new brother in Christ"?
The Church is people.

The Church is also "mission."
The Church does not exist for itself.
I think Salem Baptist is a happy church.
But is our happiness inspired by the Holy Spirit,
or is it only a social happiness?
We do many things together that are a lot of fun.
We have a basketball team that hasn't lost a game!
We all enjoy watching our men play.

We have socials where we come together and do stunts,
play games, and eat.
This kind of happiness may be caused by social compatibility
rather than spiritual oneness.
Or it can be both.

We come together for worship,
and sometimes we say the sermon was good,
the music was excellent,
everything was ordered just right.
It was worshipful, and that can make us happy.
But that kind of happiness, too, can be created
by our own social needs.

There is also a Holy Spirit happiness
that comes only when a church is on mission,
doing what it should do.
What really happened in Acts 2?
We don't know exactly, but it made an impression
on the world.
The people in Acts 2 were from different countries
and a variety of cultural backgrounds.
When the Christians came out and began to speak
and the listeners each heard someone speaking
in his own language,
they were impressed and excited.
Furthermore, the Christians were excited and happy
about the message they were giving.
That's the kind of happiness we want in the church.
It comes when we turn outward
with the message of Jesus Christ.

Sometimes we tend to blame the pastor
if not many people are being saved in the church.
But remember,
the pastor is not the Church.
You are the Church!

The pastor is part of the Church,
but together we make up the witnessing community.
Each of us must be out there explaining the Good News.
And we need to help each other learn
to do it effectively.

There are many kinds of witnesses.
This building is a witness.
It says something about the people who are in it.
Your home is a witness.
It says something about the Christ who lives in that home.
What you do at work is a witness.
Your whole life is a witness,
for *you* are the cutting edge of the Church.

The Church is meant to unite men and women
in fellowship with one another.
Maybe the word "family"
would be better than "fellowship."
A family is close-knit;
a family takes care of one another;
a family does not ignore any member.
This kind of fellowship is built on trust.
We trust one another because we have built our lives
on common truth.
Because we believe these truths,
our attitude toward each other is different.

The Church has several kinds of fellowship.
There is the fellowship of worship.
We come and worship together.
When we sing together, pray, praise, and listen together
to God's Word, we find that it meets a particular need.
On Sunday night, we use a different pattern.
We all share what is happening in our lives.
As we hear from one another,
we gain a greater sense of family solidarity.

We begin to develop a fellowship of concern.
That's a part of being God's people!
You ministered to me so deeply when I was in the hospital,
and you have continued to minister to me
every week since then.
Your children have been my ministers.
How can I tell you what it means when a child comes
to me and says, "Pastor, we pray for you every day."
A father said last week,
"I brought my son up this morning, Pastor.
He wanted to let you know that he prays for you every day,
but he is just too bashful to say so."
That is a fellowship of concern.

We are also a fellowship of people who are celebrating together.
We can enjoy the party of life.
We have come home to God
and we know what it is to enjoy the acceptance of God.
There is nothing to match the fellowship
of the Christian community.
Didn't Christ say that our love for one another
is the quality that will impress the world?

Paul tells us that the Church is a body (1 Corinthians 12:12-26).
We are many members, but we are one.
God is doing great things
through His people today.
Sometimes we tend to think of the early Church
as the perfect example,
but the Church has *never* been what God intended it to be.
It is still *becoming*.
We never dare throw out anchors and say, "Hold it!"
Let's learn to discover the eyes, the mouth,
the hands, the feet of the Church,
because when we do,
we'll move like the Church is meant to move.

If we cut off those who are a bit different from us,
or try to make them conform to our ideas,
 we miss the purpose of God.

What is the Church?
 The Church is people,
  mission,
   fellowship,
    and *the* Body of Christ.
 Christ has chosen the Church,
  His people,
   to reconcile the world to Himself.

* * *

After the service, the long line formed, through the aisles and out into the foyer, of people waiting to speak with Lin. Ten-year-old Steve came and stood by his side while he greeted the people. Rob, seven, and Scott, three, stood too for a short time each service. They were all very proud of their dad.

Although Lin was out of the hospital, he went back several times a week for tests and to have blood transfusions if necessary.

On Wednesday evening, February 21, my dad had to leave to return to California. As he left, he said in tears, "Anytime you need me, just call and I'll be on the next plane."

After he left, Lin choked back the tears, saying, "I hate to see him go. He's really the only man in my life." He had become a real father to Lin as well as to me.

My mother stayed to be of help to us. How much we needed her!

The next morning, Thursday, Lin went again for blood counts and x rays. He was feeling worse, with vomiting, fever, and drowsiness all the time. He worried that he could not study. The doctors felt that his worsening condition might be due to the drug Methotrexate, so they told him to take no more until the following Monday when they would test the blood again. His platelet count was alarmingly low. Normal count is between 200,000 and 300,000 and his was only 6,000, about one-fortieth of normal.

He had platelet transfusions and felt better. The next day Dr. Carl and Margaret Christenson had invited us to go out to dinner with them. Lin had not been out to dinner for so long that we were both looking forward to a pleasant evening. We were dressed and ready to go when Lin called to me. He had noticed blood in his urine. We called his doctor and he said to come to the hospital immediately. We asked if we could go out to dinner first. The answer was "No. Come immediately."

At the hospital he was given a blood transfusion and platelets. The doctors felt that Lin had probably been bleeding internally for some time, and it was just beginning to show.

We left Lin at the hospital and I drove home. I was discouraged but not in despair. I read Psalm 22:19: "O Thou my help, hasten to my assistance."

The next morning, Lin knew he was to have a new intern. Dr. Opsahl, with whom he had become good friends, had been transferred to another service. Lin hated the thought of having to start new with a strange doctor.

But that morning the new intern came in and said, "You don't know me, but I know you. I've been praying for you for months. I'm Tim Gess, a member of Bethlehem Baptist." It was a wonderful moment for Lin. Here was a doctor not only concerned medically, but who could share his experiences spiritually. He said that afternoon, "I guess God knew I needed someone to share with spiritually this trip. I feel quite drained."

Dr. Gess added, "You're bound to be healed with the combination of drugs and prayer!"

After recording the day's events in my diary, I added, "Good old Bud DeBar visited Lin and then took me to dinner. That was really great."

That was not the only time nor the only person who had shown that kind of consideration for me. Quite often Lin's visitors recognized my need to get away from the hospital room and share food and fellowship with Christian friends. It was a great help to my morale, and was appreciated by Lin as much as by me.

Lin had to stay in the hospital that weekend and so missed preaching on Sunday. On Tuesday evening when I went to the hospital, I took the boys along to visit their dad. When we arrived at his room, we were told that we could not go in because he was having another platelet transfusion. When the transfusion was over, he was wheeled out to a room where we could visit with him. I was shocked at his appearance. His right eye was hemorrhaging, which frightened me. But Scotty climbed up on his daddy's lap where he loved to sit. Rob and Steve asked questions about the transfusion and what it meant. Lin explained again to them that cancer is a dread disease that takes many lives each year, but that he was hopeful that the drugs would work and he would be home soon. He reminded them that we have a great God who could at any time intervene and heal him. And he also shared with them the possibility that he might be taken, but added that he hoped it wouldn't be for some time yet.

They told him about their hockey games and how much they hoped he could come home soon and see them play.

About this time, Lin received a letter from Mrs. Beverly Magnuson, a dear friend and member of Salem Church and a frequent letter writer. What she wrote expressed the feeling of many within the Salem family:

> We want you to know that we haven't forgotten you for a moment. We're hanging in there—praying, praising, and many times weeping.
>
> Last Sunday (February 25) I felt that we were going through the trauma of last August all over again. I felt impatient with God and found myself asking Him how much He can expect you (and us) to go through. "God, would You hurry up, quit stalling, and heal him?"
>
> I'm getting angry, knowing God can heal you and my feeling that He is refusing to. I have not asked God why He had let you get sick. But instead I find myself asking, "Why haven't You healed him?" So I guess I'm not as mature as I thought I was. I *know* and *believe* many things, but along comes a flood of emotion to drown out all my reasoning.
>
> I have no problem in knowing what to pray for. I am begging God for your complete healing. A passage in Daniel that really comforts me: "For we do not present our supplications before thee on the ground of our righteousness, but on the ground of thy great mercy" (Dan. 9: 18*b*).*
>
> If I thought your healing depended on my prayers being just right or my life being righteous, I'd lose my mind. I wouldn't want to live if I thought that God could not or would not heal you because of the frailty of my faith. I don't think God plays games like that with us. . . .
>
> We know, as you do, that God is good. We want to love and serve Him, come what may. We love the Karo family so much it hurts! Some days I'm sure it must be *easier* to *hate,* because this caring has sure been painful!
>
> LOVE YOU DEAR PEOPLE,
> BEV AND NORRIS

*RSV.

12
For All the Saints

By March 1 it was evident that the longed-for remission was not taking place, but the pendulum still swung between hope and despair.

Lin had earlier written, "We really could not exist without hope. I have been told that I have perhaps a year to live. What do I hope for that year? My first hope is that I will have *more* than one year, and I pray that God will give me more time. And I dig in my heels to resist this disease. I believe that disease is evil, foreign to the creation of God. Christ resisted death—He prayed that the cup might pass from Him. I do not think it is wrong to resist death or to dislike it. I hope that God will intervene and destroy this evil disease. But I have another hope given by the Bible that someday things will be different. Disease will be no more; those who have died will be resurrected, and together we will share life. Those who are dying can know that someday they will be gathered with those in the Lord whom they love. This brings a great sense of confidence."

Early in the morning of March 1, Lin had a deep spiritual experience with God. He again laid before the Lord his whole frustrating experience with cancer. As he prayed, he realized that God, after all, still was there and in control of the situation. But he struggled and wept at the thought of dying before his boys were grown. He told God he really wanted to stay until his boys reached maturity. He told me later that this was the first time the reality had hit him so hard.

As he contemplated the possibility of death, he was thankful for the financial provisions he had made for his family. At the cost of some financial struggle a few years earlier, he had set up a good insurance program to care for me and the boys. Money from his retirement program would come to us. That, with social security benefits, would permit us to live modestly but adequately. He had enrolled in an excellent health-insurance program that was now meeting his astronomical hospital bills.

Knowing that he had planned well gave him some satisfaction, but it did not lessen his struggle with death. In our talks together he had indicated the intensity of his struggle and his confidence that God is good and He knew exactly what he was going through. That thought obsessed him: God was with him.

He also indicated how glad he was that he had lived his life as he had. "I like the way I've lived," he said, "and there are very few things I would do differently if I had it to do again. I enjoy being a minister; I see people who have been changed through the Gospel as I have proclaimed it, and that is a great privilege."

When the medical reports came in on March 1, there were some encouraging signs. His white-blood count had come down to 900, and showed only 25 percent malignant cells. On the previous day, the count had been much higher.

Dr. Carl Christenson later told me that Lin's blood counts became a matter of deep interest to many hospital people. Dr. Christenson's residence specialty was in surgery so he would normally have no contact with Lin and his illness, but because of their close personal friendship he kept constant contact with Lin's case.

And from Carl's inside view of the hospital, he could see the influence that Lin was having on hospital personnel.

Carl said, "You never had to go very far to find out what Lin's condition was. I could ask in the dining hall at the hospital or on any floor within ten minutes after the blood counts had been determined, and there would be someone there who knew what today's count was. Yet, this was a huge hospital (515 beds). But nearly everyone seemed to know about and love Lin—the administrators, janitors, doctors, nurses. When things were bad for him, they all suffered. They seemed to be living and dying with him.

"Lindon permeated St. Paul Ramsey Hospital. Everyone questioned one another as to his present condition. Most of the doctors made their rounds for their own responsibilities, and then we all came and made rounds of Lin. Most of the medical staff seemed to keep constant check on his chart. He allowed young doctors to come in and talk candidly and comfortably.

"Probably one of the main reasons for this intense interest," he noted, "was that Lin was demonstrating that death was a manageable subject even for a young person. In spite of his own intense struggle, he displayed that 'I can be a happy, meaningful, viable person.'

"He could and did talk to them about the meaning of death and the meaning of the Christian faith. It was a potent lesson in dying with the Christian perspective. One person said to me, 'He really is some sort of guy to manage this and relate to it.'

"The staff seemed captivated by Lindon, perhaps because they felt their need to learn the lesson he had already conquered. He had an intelligent understanding of his medical situation. Toward the end, the black news seemed to get worse day after day, but he swallowed it and went on as the bright spirit he was. I have been a practicing physician for twenty years, and I have never seen anyone manage an illness like this with the degree of Christian spirit he had.

"It became difficult for the physicians who knew him to accept his situation. We work with people who have been in accidents and who die. But this seemed different and the question that kept haunting all of us was, 'Why, God? Why a young man with everything going for him? Can't You intervene for this young man?'

"The personal involvement in his case was intense, and he helped all of us learn how to confront death."

Although Lindon's condition was precarious, he wanted to go home and preach on Sunday. And so, on March 3, with the help and persuasion of Dr. Timothy Gess, the new intern, the doctors agreed to give him a weekend pass.

By the time he was released, his white count had fallen to the dangerous level of 400 (normal 5,000 to 10,000), the platelet count was only 12,000 (about *one-twentieth* of normal), and hemoglobin was a low 8.8. But they were letting him go home to preach. He was delighted.

As a part of the full house on that Sunday morning, March 4, were two doctors and two nurses from St. Paul Ramsey Hospital. He had to be helped to the platform and to his chair. His face was ashen. One of the members later commented that when she saw him there, she thought, *The doctors have given up. That's why they let him come.*

It was his last sermon. It was especially meaningful to him because he felt so deeply that the body of believers (saints) had given him real communion, concern, prayer, and support in his struggle with death.

* * *

I Believe in the Communion of the Saints

It is good to be back with you today.
One frustrating complication is with me this morning.
I see two of each of you.
I had a hemorrhage in the most sensitive spot in the right eye.
My left eye pulls things over a bit
and as a result I see two of you.

I miss being with God's people; you mean so much to me.
The Christian community is different
from any other community in the world.
That's what the creed speaks of
as the "communion of the saints."

The well-known psychiatrist, William Glasser,
has written a book called *The Identity Society*.
He says that we have passed through
what he calls the "civilized survival society,"
which has lasted from about 10,000 years ago to 1950.
Until about 1950, man's primary struggle was to survive.
He was absorbed with questions like,
"What is going to be my occupation?
How am I going to care for a family?
How am I going to be a success?"
But about 1950, Glasser says, something changed
and the primary question for most people became
"Who am I?
I want to know my identity
and I want to be a part of a society,
a group, a community,
where people are discovering who they are."

Actually, this thinking posed another question:
"Where do I find such a community?
Where are people discovering who they are?
And are they enjoying what they are discovering?"

In the midst of this newly felt need
sits the community of saints,
God's people.
We are discovering who we are;
we are discovering the meaning of life,
and we celebrate that meaning together.

Perhaps that word "saint" bothers you a bit
because we have given it the wrong connotation.
It was meant to be an earthy term
applied to people who are *struggling*
to achieve spiritual goals.

The New Testament use of "saint" suggests a person
who has asked "Who am I?"
and discovered some things he didn't like—
that he was self-centered and independent.
He didn't like what he saw
and asked, "Is that really me?"

And God answered him through His Word,
or through other means,
"Yes, that's you.
Your concerns are centered around yourself,
and your eyes have not been opened to people or to Me.
You may say you believe in Me,
but you have never asked Me to deliver you
from your self-centered, independent existence
and to liberate you through Jesus Christ.
Christ has atoned for your sins of self-centeredness,
and I want you to enter a new kind of life.
I want to make you a saint."

When we embark on the road to sainthood,
we become a part of a community of saints,
and we discover another dimension,
a kind of life for one another.

We soon learn that this is a caring community.
In Acts 2:44-45 there is an interesting account
about the early experiences of the Church:

> All those who had believed were together, and had all things in common; and they began selling their property and possessions, and were sharing them with all, as any one might have need.

Later in Acts 4:34-35 there is this comment:

> There was not a needy person among them, for all who were owners of lands or houses would sell them and bring the proceeds of the sales, and lay them at the apostles' feet; and they would be distributed to each, as any had need.

Something had happened to make these people say,
"I care so much for you
that I will sell what I have
and give to any of you who is in need."

I don't think the Scriptures are telling all of us
to sell everything we have
and start distributing to one another.
In our society that would not necessarily demonstrate love.
Our American pride
sometimes makes it hard for us to accept help.
We want to be self-sufficient.

This troubles me in regard to my cancer.
I can't walk as I used to.
I need help to get from one place to another,
and I find it humiliating.
It is not only more blessed to give than to receive;
it is also easier.
If we are aware of this,
it will help us to guard the dignity
of those we seek to help.

I had a bad experience one day this week in the hospital.
My right eye was hemorrhaging,
and they wanted me to go down to the eye clinic
and have it checked out.
I waited two and one-half hours
in the hallway in a wheelchair.
Nobody seemed to care about me
or others waiting there.

Finally, I was examined and began to leave.
In the process I got into a different-colored wheelchair
than the one that was assigned to the seventh floor.
Suddenly a nurse came running after us, saying,
"I have to have this wheelchair back.
It belongs here."
At that moment I felt that they were more concerned
about their wheelchair than the patient in it.

But we easily fall into the same sin.
We tend to care more about possessions
than we care about people.
The early Christians didn't only *say* they were God's people;
they showed it
by selling what they had
and distributing it as people had need.

In our congregation and community,
our greatest needs probably are not material.
But we have other kinds of needs
that we should know and respond to.
The way you have responded to me
shows you are a caring congregation.
Your loving spirit has not been limited to me.
Some of you have responded to the special needs
of foreign students in our area.
Some of you have given many hours
and opened your homes and family life
to these people who are often lonely.

You do it because your own lives have been touched by God.
Saints are caring people.

Saints are not only a caring people;
they are a sharing community.
Galatians 6:2-5 reads:

> Bear one another's burdens, and thus fulfill the law of Christ. For if anyone thinks he is something when he is nothing, he deceives himself. But let each one examine his own work, and then he will have reason for boasting in regard to himself alone, and not in regard to another. For each one shall bear his own load.

Let me tell you how I think this works.
When Lee Eliason, our associate pastor, comes to visit me in the hospital, we share together.
Sometimes I share my frustrations—and my joys.
But when Lee leaves,
even though I know he bears my burden with me,
it is still my burden.
It may be easier to carry
because I have a fellow saint who shares it.
But I still have to pick it up and carry it.

I was converted as a teenager.
I remember one experience when I was very young in Christ.
I was talking with the young man
who led me to receiving Christ.
There was one particular sin that greatly troubled me.
I shared this with him,
and found that as a young man he had the same problem.
We agreed to pray for one another.
He also became a pastor, and to this day
there is a special bond between us.
We discovered, through reading Scripture
and praying together,
the right course for our lives, because we shared together.

Some of you are going through experiences that weigh heavily.
Some of you have carried a burden for years,
and you wonder if God really has forgiven you.
Probably more than anything else
you need a fellow saint to say,
"I love you, accept you,
and don't look down on you
for what you have done in the past."
The only way some Christians can experience
the real forgiveness
of God is to hear a fellow saint say that.
We can mediate the forgiveness of God to others.
In the process we may need the mediating presence of God
to give us humility
and integrity
never to pass on to others the particular problem
someone is sharing.

Of course, we must remember that sharing is a two-way street.
Some of you have never had anyone share
a genuine spiritual problem with you.
Perhaps you are wondering why.
The Scriptures say, "Bear one another's burden."
You cannot bear someone else's burden
unless you are willing to share yours.
As you begin to share your burden,
you will find those who will say,
"I need help, too, in the same area."
As you *share* your burden,
you begin to *bear* others' burdens.
That's what the community of the saints is about.

I used to be afraid of hugging another man,
probably because I was fearful of what others would think.
But some of the greatest experiences in the hospital
have come when men of this church,
with tears in their eyes, came in and hugged me.

That action carried a message.
It said, "We don't like what's happening to you,
and we love you."
I felt so close to those men.
Some of you may need that kind of expression.

We all need someone to affirm us.
I remember the Sunday in September
I came back to preach after my first treatments for cancer.
The first lady to come out at the close of the service,
kissed me and said, "I love you,"
and walked out.
Oh, did that mean something!
To this day, that person is very special to me.
Now, I don't really expect all the women to kiss me,
even though that would be very nice, as I need affirmation.
Actually, today I have orders to leave immediately
after the sermon.
I won't even be able to say hi to you.

I must say one more thing about the communion of saints.
It is a complete community.
Baptists don't make up all the saints in the world.
There are a lot of saints around;
we find some of them in the Catholic church,
in the Lutheran church,
in the Covenant church.
They are all a part of the community of the saints,
and we are finally discovering each other.
We are a part of the communion of saints.

I discover saints in the hospital.
When I had to go back to the hospital
two and one-half weeks ago,
I was discouraged.
I said to the Lord, "Why? Why, again?
I am really getting tired of this, Lord.

Just when I think that we are getting somewhere,
something crops up someplace else."
So many problems have come with the treatment
that I was beginning to think that the treatment
was worse than the disease.
I was upset with it all.

Then I found that my intern,
who had cared for me for three months,
was transferred to another department.
I was unhappy about beginning with a new intern.
But this new man walked in and said,
"You don't know me, but I feel I really know you.
I have been praying for you for months."
I could have jumped out of that bed.
He said, "I am a member of Bethlehem Baptist Church."
He said he attended a prayer meeting
where some of the interns get together on Thursday nights.
"And we never forget you," he said.
God sent the man I needed.
I said, "God, I'm sorry that I got so upset.
You had somebody special for me."

You find saints all over–
men and women and children who are doing their job.
They love people,
care for people.
That's the communion of saints
of which you are a part.
William Glasser says our society needs people
who have learned to identify themselves.
I say the only people who can really identify themselves
are the saints
because they are becoming what God intended them to be.

It is great to be a saint
and to have communion with one another.

It is holy communion,
a special type of communion
set apart for the people of God.

* * *

Lin was due to return to the hospital on Monday morning, and by that time even he had to admit that he belonged in the hospital. As he tried to dress, the dizziness was so great that he had to lie down, getting up in little spurts to get a shirt on, or some buttons fastened. Then he began vomiting. We finally got to the hospital, but it was a miserable day. In the evening, Pastor Art Rouner came again from Colonial church. He really lifted Lin's spirits, and his prayer with Lin was considerate, meaningful, loving.

Daily tests showed little change until Thursday when the results of the last bone-marrow test were brought in. It showed that the marrow was packed with malignant cells. When Dr. Taddeini brought us this news, he also mentioned that he had just learned that the cancer research budget of the federal government had been cut 25 percent. I was so upset that while Lin rested that afternoon, I scribbled a note to President Nixon, telling him that I thought human life ought to have priority over moon missions.

By Friday, the medical picture was slightly more encouraging, with the white-cell count going up and the percentage of malignant cells going down. He was given a transfusion of platelets and after that he felt somewhat better, so we decided to play chess.

Lin always won in chess and this day, as usual, I was losing. Dr. Taddeini walked in and asked how I was doing; then he looked at the board and saw for himself. He stood there awhile, giving me suggestions, and finally sat down on Lin's bed, took over my men, and really gave Lin a good game. After a while, when he had so improved my position that he thought I could win, he left the game to me. I still lost! But it stood out to me as another act by a busy doctor to show care and concern for Lin and me during this difficult time.

Lin hoped he could be released to preach on Sunday, March 11, but he began developing other complications, this time in his ears. They would not permit him to leave the hospital. After the evening service at Salem, Pastor Lee Eliason came to visit Lin. Just the three of us were there, and we talked about heaven. It was a conversation full of humor as well as seriousness, and at times we laughed hilariously at some of our ideas. Lin said he thought of heaven as a place where people would continue to grow and develop. "It is not going to be an 11 o'clock worship service extending for all eternity!"

Lin mentioned that when Christ came to earth, He learned what it was like to be man. I wondered whether in heaven, we might learn to know what it was to be God. We were able to question, theorize, and not worry about orthodox interpretation or being rejected by each other.

Lee later commented, "Lin was thoroughly orthodox in beliefs he would share from the pulpit. But when he was with me or with Emmett Johnson or with you, he would think out loud, trying to make sense of some of the most difficult biblical truths. He let his mind travel in any direction to explore new ideas. In our conversation about heaven, we all knew that the Bible didn't spell out very much, so we were all reaching out together for possible ideas and evaluating them. I appreciated Lin's willingness to do this."

That conversation about heaven was deeply meaningful to Lin because he was able to share, to laugh, and to realize that heaven will be a great place.

A few days before his death, he had a similar conversation with Emmett Johnson. They talked about the fact that heaven would not be wearing angels' robes and wings. Lin wondered whether the new heaven and new earth might not be here in some kind of fifth dimension. They talked about how hung up people become with concepts of golden streets and a four-square city. They agreed that these things express that heaven is another existence.

They kidded about what they would do when they got to heaven. Lin said he planned to study a lot. He would read and dispute with Paul, because Paul was a scholar of the first rate.

He said he was not afraid of death, although he would rather live than die. And then he said to all of us—Emmett, my dad, and me—"What bothers me is that I'll probably get there before you do."

* * *

By now the long months of emotional ups and downs, unending trips to the hospital, and trying to maintain some degree of normalcy in the lives of our boys had left me emotionally and physically drained. I was so thankful that my mother was staying with me. I could leave the children and the house in her care while I made my daily treks to the hospital.

Now, to add to my troubles, we began having serious car troubles, and I realized that I was now responsible for many problems that Lin had always cared for in the past. I tried reminding myself of others in similar or worse situations. But although these things helped, my greatest encouragement was from the Bible, especially the Psalms. I found Psalm 73:16 especially helpful:

> So I set myself to think this out
> but I found it too hard for me,
> until I went into God's sacred courts;
> there I saw clearly what their end would be (NEB).

And He always met me there. I prayed, "It seems I keep getting reassured in Your Word. Let me cling to that. I need it tonight."

That night I read Psalm 18:1-6:

> I love thee, O LORD my strength.
> The LORD is my stronghold, my fortress and my
> champion,
> my God, my rock where I find safety,
> my shield, my mountain refuge, my strong tower.
> I will call on the LORD to whom all praise is due,
> and I shall be delivered from my enemies.
> When the bonds of death held me fast,
> destructive torrents overtook me,
> the bonds of Sheol tightened round me,
> the snares of death were set to catch me;
> then in anguish of heart I cried to the LORD,
> I called for help to my God;
> he heard me from his temple,
> and my cry reached his ears (NEB).

And sleep came easily.

Bud DeBar was carrying more and more of the church responsibility. Instead of consulting with Lin about major decisions concerning the church, the church board made the decisions and Bud reported to Lin what was happening. He knew Lin's deep desire to be out of the hospital weekends to preach, and he tried to let Lin keep all his strength for that.

Lin, like all the rest of us, tried to balance the realism of the medical reports with hope and faith in God's intervention. He felt that he must know all the medical facts and that he must be prepared to die. He once said, "This is one of the most difficult things to grasp. You must face the facts, but you cannot become fatalistic or give up. We really cannot exist without hope."

Others recognized, too, the need to maintain hope with and for Lin. One day a couple came into Lin's room laden with boxes. They were bringing a gift from the Twin City North Area pastors of the Minnesota Baptist Conference. Lin opened the boxes and found a new sport coat, pants, shirt, and tie. It was their gesture of confidence that God was going to heal him and that he would be able to wear them.

Lin and I talked openly and freely about his cancer, about the possibility of his dying, but always with the knowledge that God *could* heal either with or without drugs.

As his situation worsened, Lin asked me, *not if,* but "Will you stay in New Brighton? Will you rent an apartment, or buy a house? Will you marry again? Will it be a pastor?" I had thought through the first two questions back in August, so I was able to answer with conviction. I would stay in New Brighton and buy a house. I wasn't prepared to answer the question about marrying again. I told him that and added that I loved being a pastor's wife.

Lin was scheduled to be released on Tuesday, March 13, but during the night he developed fever and chills. Shortly after I arrived we received the medical reports: only 200 white cells and only 1,000 platelets. That was the worst report we had ever received. He was placed immediately in protective isolation. While Lin slept, I called Ardi Carlson, a neighbor and a member of Salem and asked her to begin the church prayer chain on Lin's behalf. It was a method by which each person in the church directory called the next person in the directory to alert him or her of special prayer needs. I knew that the church family would soon be in special prayer for Lin.

I wanted to read Scripture while Lin lay there sleeping, but I was too emotionally distraught to concentrate. God's

Word had been my strength, but at this time I could not read. That afternoon I wrote in my diary, "I can't read. I want to use this time to pray, God. I want to cry out loud to You, but I can't because Lin will see and hear me and be more upset. I want to struggle with this until I know what You have for us. I feel very, very unholy and unpious and quite sinful, and I don't know why. Perhaps because I stand before a very holy God. I want to humble myself before You, and yet I don't really know what that means. I'll struggle here quietly and thank You that You are here. Make me completely aware of that now."

I did reach the conclusion that God indeed *can* heal. He is not limited to drugs or diet or even my prayer.

Lin's temperature kept rising that day. At 9 o'clock that night they began intravenous antibiotics. That night I read from Psalm 56:9-13 (NEB) : "For this I know, that God is on my side, with God to help me I will shout defiance . . . for thou hast rescued me from death to walk in thy presence, in the light of life." And then in Psalm 57:1*b* (NEB), "I will take refuge in the shadow of thy wings until the storms are past."

The next day, Wednesday, March 14, Dr. Carl Christenson called and said he wanted to take me to lunch. I went to the hospital early to spend time with Lin before I went to lunch. He was very ill. His fever had gone down slightly; but antibiotics were still being pumped into him, and it was more difficult to get from his bed to the bathroom. If I was there, I helped him; otherwise he needed assistance from hospital personnel. He asked me to call my dad and ask him to come. I promised that I would do so.

I felt uneasy about my coming luncheon with Carl. Intuitively I knew he was going to bring me bad news, and I had my guard up. My intuition was right. He tried to tell me that Lin's situation looked very grim. I heard what he said with my ears, but I refused to relinquish my hope. After all, he had told me something similar last October, and Lin had rallied after that. Carl apparently realized what I was doing, and he asked me to go and visit Dr. Taddeini after lunch.

He walked with me into Dr. Taddeini's office and left me there. Facing this doctor who had been so kind to me and to Lin, I finally brought myself to ask the important question. "How long do you think Lin has?"

He did not answer me directly but gently explained that the bone marrow was no longer producing cells for the blood and the drugs were not working. When I pressed him further as to how long Lin would live, he finally answered, "Two weeks at the most; only days if infection sets in."

I struggled to hold back the tears. "Can I take him home then?"

Dr. Taddeini thought for a moment and then said, "You really wouldn't be able to handle his needs at home."

I left the office and *ran* down seven flights of stairs. I didn't want to risk meeting anyone in the elevator. I found a phone and called home where my mother was caring for Scotty. Between sobs I told her the story and asked her to find Dad, who had been traveling down to southern California on his way to visit my sister in Phoenix.

Finally I was able to gain enough composure to go back to Lin's room. Lin had not been told that the case was medically hopeless, and the doctors felt that he needed all the hope he could have.

That Wednesday was one of the longest days of my life. I tried to hide my tears and act normal, but inside I was being torn apart. Later in that afternoon as Lin slept, I read 2 Corinthians 4:16-18:

> No wonder we do not lose heart! Though our outward humanity is in decay, yet day by day we are inwardly renewed. Our troubles are slight and short-lived; and their outcome an eternal glory which outweighs them far. Meanwhile our eyes are fixed, not on the things that are seen, but on the things that are unseen: for what is seen passes away; what is unseen is eternal (NEB).

And God was there.

Later in the afternoon while Lin slept, I called Emmett Johnson. I felt I had to talk with someone. He promised to come to the hospital in the evening. Lin loved to have Emmett visit. By the time he came, Lin was feeling better and I was calmer.

However, the days seemed to be piling up burden after burden, more than I could possibly bear. We now learned that Lin's mother was in the hospital in California, scheduled soon for surgery for an abdominal tumor. The doctors said it could be malignant, but they thought and hoped it would be benign. Surgery was set for the following Monday, March 19. I had told Lin about this, and his concern for her was very deep. But she could under no circumstances come now to see Lin.

On Thursday, March 15, Lin was feeling better than he had the day before. He wanted so much to get out of the hospital and preach on Sunday, but he realized he was too weak to do so. In the afternoon, Lin repeated his desire, "I wish your dad would come." When I told him that Dad would be here by the weekend, he wept in joy.

That day I cried with every visitor who came. I would go with the visitors to the coffee shop and weep with them. Then I would go back to 7 South and thank God that I and all visitors had to wear gowns and masks, for the masks somewhat hid my beady-red eyes.

That evening the phone rang in Lin's room. It was my

dad calling from my sister Judy's home in Scottsdale. Lin told him how thankful he was that he was coming and related his experience of the afternoon, and both men began to cry. Finally Lin handed me the phone and said, "You talk. You are the only one in control here." He didn't realize that because I was "cried out" I was now able to be more in control.

Later that evening, I felt that I had to tell Lin what the doctor had told me. My dad was coming with full knowledge of the medical facts; others knew them; I felt he had to know. So I told him, "The bone marrow has quit producing; the drugs are no longer effective." It was a dark and bleak hour. Lin wept. He said, "I can't leave the boys, Steve and Rob and little Scotty." Whenever Lin was home, he spent hours holding Scotty, then three, on his lap. Scotty idolized his daddy. He would pray, "Thank You, Jesus, for Daddy, and for Daddy's hospital. I want Daddy home. Thank You, for he won't have to take no more medicines. A-em."

Lin and I wept together that night, holding each other tight—mask and all. Then Lin said, "We'll have to go on from here. There is nothing we can do about it." He did not leave out the possibility of divine intervention. We clung to that hope. God had sustained us throughout these months. We struggled, cried, shared our feelings, our frustrations, and our love for each other.

I stayed at the hospital that night, sleeping on the bed next to Lin, with my mask on. He woke several times during the night in pain and needing assistance to the bathroom. But he called the nurse, not wanting to disturb me. As uncomfortable as I was with that silly mask on, I did sleep and did not hear him when he awakened. Perhaps that was all I needed—to be near him.

He said later that even though he didn't awaken me,

just having the one you love near you during this difficult time was sufficient.

In the morning I woke early, ate breakfast, and drove to the airport to meet Dad. When we arrived at the hospital, Dad almost ran into Lin's room and embraced him; and then they were both crying. I stood by watching the two dearest men in my life weeping with each other. Dad stayed with Lin the entire day. By evening, Lin was looking better.

The next day I received a letter from a dear friend, Nancy Baumann, that gave more encouragement to Lin as to the influence he had had.

> I had another argument with the Lord this week. I said, "Lord, we believe and *are* asking in Your name. Why isn't Lin being healed? Hundreds are praying, not just two or three. And if it is not Your will for healing, why so much up and down? I know the longer he is with people, the more lives are being touched, but these letdowns are too much. Then, Lord, the timing is all wrong. He just came to Salem; he is young; he is needed by three young sons and a wife who loves her role. Why have this happen now? Why not ten years from now? Think of the seminary students he influences. I think of two who came to Salem bitter; but after being with Lin six months, they left to have their own churches and excited about the ministry. . . . Why now?" Then I was reminded of a definition of faith: "recognizing that God is the Lord of time when my timing doesn't agree with His." I had to stop and remember that I worship God for who He is and not what He does or allows.

On Saturday, March 17, Dad spent the day with Lin at the hospital while I took Steve to his hockey game and did some errands. About 4:30 in the afternoon, I brought Steve to see Lin. The other boys had such bad colds that I did not dare bring them. Steve was anxious to see his dad, yet apprehensive. He asked me, "What will we do if Dad dies?" I explained that God could still heal Dad, but if He did not, Dad had planned well and we would be cared for. The nursing station had garb ready for Steve. He was quite a sight, with a backless hospital gown hanging loosely on him and with a protective mask made for a large face. Steve had said he wanted to talk to his father alone, so Dad and I stepped out of the room, leaving the two alone to talk.

On Sunday, March 18, I went to the hospital to stay with Lin for the day rather than going to church. Emmett Johnson had given me a book to read, *How to Tell Your Child About Death,* which I finished reading while Lin slept. I prayed much for Lin, for us, for his mother who would have surgery in the morning. I felt deeply for her. Her son was dying in a hospital in Minnesota while she had surgery in California.

On Monday we were told that Elim Baptist Church in Anoka was having a twenty-four-hour-a-day prayer chain for Lin's healing. At times when we were discouraged, God sent bits of encouragement through His people to lift us up.

In the afternoon we got a telephone call saying that Lin's mother had come through surgery OK and the tumors were benign.

On Tuesday there were more tests and transfusions. By evening Lin's temperature began rising. Dad was getting more concerned and taking more nitroglycerin tablets for his heart. I didn't know whom to worry about the most!

On Tuesday night when I returned home, I was utterly exhausted both physically and emotionally. Before I fell asleep, I turned again to the Psalms and I came to Psalm 68:5, I read, "father of the fatherless, the widow's champion—God in his holy dwelling-place" (NEB).

"O God," I prayed, "don't let this be prophetic."

When I arrived at the hospital on Wednesday, it was obvious to me that Lin was not only a very sick man but a dying man. He talked very little and was in such discomfort that he finally asked for a hypo.

But I could tell that he was so glad we were there. And I thought of something that he had written back in November when he hoped he would be able to write a book about his experience with cancer and death. "Although in a very deep sense every man must meet his own death alone, he cannot endure the experience alone. Everyone facing death needs a group of friends to stand with him. Friends bring something on the human level that cannot be given any other way."

He had also written, "But we need support from *more* than the human level, too. A man facing death must know that God is *for* him. God knows exactly what I'm going through. There is no one else who can help us as God can. God is very good."

Although he did not talk much, he obviously was alert to all that was going on around him. Dr. Christenson, who was in and out of the room much of the day, was astonished at how clear his mind was. At one point, Lin suggested that my dad and I play Scrabble, because he liked the sound of people talking around him.

Emmett Johnson and Lee Eliason both stayed with us to the end. Early in the evening, Lee bent over and said, "We love you, brother"; and Lin answered back, "I love you, Lee."

We all knew that we were facing the end, and so did Lin. He chided us for our apparent sadness. When Gordy Lindquist came in the room in the early evening, knowing that Lin was dying, Lin said to him, "Why are you guys so gloomy?"

Our grief was shared by the hospital staff. Dr. Tim Gess, Lin's Christian intern, sat at the nursing station most of the afternoon, tears streaming down his face.

About 9:45 that evening, Lin leaned over to me and said, "Good-bye, honey." Then he grabbed Dad's hand and said, "Thanks for coming, Lloyd." And to Emmett, "It's been great, Emmett." A few minutes later he said, "I wanted to go in a blaze of glory, but this is the best I can do." He lapsed into a coma.

Lindon Peder Karo died at 10:40 P.M., March 21, at the age of thirty-two. He did not live to preach the last two sermons, "I Believe in the Resurrection of the Body," and "I Believe in the Life Everlasting." But he is experiencing both.

* * *

The morning after Lin's death, I called Steve and Rob into my room and told them that Daddy was now in heaven with Jesus. Between their tears, the boys asked questions. Later three-year-old Scotty came in. "We have to bury Daddy, don't we?" was his first question.

I answered, "Yes, we do. Why?"

"Because Daddy is in heaven with Jesus. We can't visit Daddy in the hospital anymore. If we want to visit Daddy, we have to go to heaven with Jesus." And he left the room.

I sent the boys to school that day and then called the school to explain what had happened and asked that the boys be permitted to come home if they wanted to.

When they arrived home that afternoon, Steve said he did not want to go to school the next day. "The kids are asking me so many questions, and I don't know how to answer them."

In Rob's class, I later learned, the children had been asked to write a letter to a classmate who was in the hospital. Rob told his teacher that he could not do that. He wanted to write a letter to his dad. On the outside he wrote, "To Dad. From Robby." On the inside was a picture of a boy with tears running down from his face to a puddle of tears on the ground. Underneath, it said, "I wish you didn't die, Dad. I didn't want you to die."

Steve stayed home the next day, but Rob went to school. Steve and I went shopping for clothes for the boys. On the way, he said to me, "You know, Mom, Job suffered. He *really* suffered, but he still believed God." I was taken aback by his statement. He sounded so much like Lin, and, of course, he looked so much like Lin. I felt Steve would do OK. I thanked God for a Sunday school teacher who studied the book of Job with ten-year-olds and who had not been afraid to use Steve's dad as an illustration. Now, when he really needed it, Steve could draw on what he had learned.

We received hundreds of comforting cards and letters. But one spoke so deeply to me that I asked the church secretary to reproduce it and include it with the worship folder for the Salem congregation on Sunday, March 25.

> DEAR NANCY,
>
> We have heard that Lindon departed to "be with Christ" which has been described as being "far better." For most of us, locked in our earth-bound understanding, this is a hard experience. What words can we say? Hesitantly, because I do not know what to say, I share with you a dialogue of my mind.
>
> "But Lord, why?"
>
> > "I once asked that question in the days of my flesh, and all I had for a reply was a blackened sky. It is not for you to know now; you could not understand."
>
> "It does not make sense. We needed him. The church needed him."

"No. No. You need *me!* Have I not said I will never fail you or forsake you?"

"But we loved him."

"Do you think I don't?"

"We know You do. But we prayed so hard."

"So did I. Have you forgotten my prayer? 'Father, I desire that they also, whom thou hast given me, may be with me where I am, to behold my glory which thou hast given me in thy love for me before the foundation of the world.' "

"All that is so much beyond us, Lord. We are only human. What do You expect of us?"

"That you trust me. No one ever found me an empty cup or a barren land. 'My sheep hear my voice, and I know them, and they follow me; and I give them eternal life, and they shall never perish, and no one shall snatch them out of my hand.' "

There is nothing I could say that has not been said a thousand times, and that will not probably be said to you by others in the next few days. We just wanted you to know that our prayers will be added to all their prayers for you.

Phil. 1:23; Heb. 13:5*b*;

John 17:24; John 10:27-28 (RSV)

Sincerely in Christ,

John Hoeldtke
Pastor,
Olivet Baptist Church

That Sunday morning service was a difficult one, I am told. The church was packed again with people who were hurting deeply. I suppose in microcosm they had gone through much of my experience—the despair, hope, desperate praying, searching for a word from God that Lin would be healed, the battering on the doors of heaven, the deep desire to say "Thy will be done" but the resistance to thinking that death could be God's will.

Just as Lin did not want to face death alone, so I did not want to face sorrow alone. And the knowledge that there were hundreds of people grieving with me did give support and comfort in those desolate hours when I could only think of how much I loved him and that he was gone.

The funeral service was set for Monday afternoon and the reviewal on Sunday from 3 to 9 P.M. On Saturday evening my parents and I and the boys went to the funeral home. Scotty stared at Lin's body, finally patted his stomach, and said, "This is Daddy's body." He seemed to understand that Daddy was gone.

When Rob came to the casket, he slipped into Lin's pocket the "letter to Daddy" that he had written at school. That was almost more than I could bear.

I wondered how I would be able to function at the reviewal, but it proved to be a day of healing for me. With some, I was able to laugh; I wept with many. I would never have understood how important that time was. Even when people didn't know what to say or didn't say a word, it showed that they cared for Lin and for me.

I was glad that I had planned the funeral service back in October when the emotional pressure was not so great. We had the condensation of his September 3 sermon, "I Believe in God," printed and distributed at the funeral. The church was jammed and included nearly one hundred pastors from Minnesota. At the close of the service, they formed a chorus and sang "To God Be the Glory." The choir sang "Eternal Life," the prayer of Saint Francis of Assisi that had been used as a benediction each Sunday since October. The congregation sang "For All the Saints." But the most meaningful portion was the sharing time.

A sharing time had become a regular part of the Sunday evening service at Salem. Lin would always say, "Let's hear what has happened to the family of God this past week." And it seemed right that this closing service of his ministry should include such a time. One woman stood to tell how she had become a Christian through hearing the tape of his September 3 message. A seminary student said he wanted to pattern his life and preaching after Lin's. Several of the men of the church stood to tell of the impact that Lin's life had made on them.

Through the months of Lin's illness, I had often stood on Sunday night to tell how the Lord was sustaining me and dealing with me. I wanted to say something on this occasion too, and I prayed for composure to be able to do so. God answered my prayer, and I was able to stand and say something like this: "Lin talked so much of God holding his hand. Psalm 63:8 (NEB) says, 'I humbly follow thee with all my heart, and thy right hand is my support.' I feel God holding *my* hand now. I loved being a pastor's wife, and I was especially proud to be Lindon Karo's wife."

The message, "Thoughts on Heaven," was given by the Reverend Emmett Johnson who had been so close to Lin during his illness and who had been with us as we watched Lin leave this world.

* * *

Thoughts on Heaven

> Set your troubled hearts at rest. Trust in God always; trust also in me. There are many dwelling-places in my Father's house; if it were not so I should have told you; for I am going there on purpose to prepare a place for you. And if I go and prepare a place for you, I shall come again and receive you to myself, so that where I am you may be also; and my way there is known to you. Thomas said, "Lord, we do not know where you are going, so how can we know the way?" Jesus

replied, "I am the way; I am the truth and I am life; no one comes to the Father except by me" (John 14:1-6, NEB).

I don't know when I have seen so many people
preoccupied with the life and death of a man:
the people of Salem Baptist,
who knew him so well and loved him so much;
the Bethel Seminary community, who respected him;
the staff of St. Paul Ramsey Hospital,
who admired him;
the churches of the Baptist General Conference
and especially pastors of the Minnesota Baptist Conference
(there are over one hundred of them present today),
who in their deep concern for a brother
continually asked me, "How is Lindon?"

His impending death seemed so tragic,
basically because he was one of our best pastors
and most able speakers;
he was young,
he was a family man,
he was dying of cancer.

There have been troubled hearts these days.
Why didn't he live?
We don't know why God did not overrule
and vanquish death.
But we do know that in his dying,
Lindon's life and witness
(as well as Nancy's) were powerful.
He taught us how to live
and how to die.
He showed no bitterness.
He was a man of God through it all.

Just a few hours before he died, he looked at us
who stood by and said,
with that characteristic twinkle in his eye:

"You know, I thought I was going to go out
in a blaze of glory.
but this is the best I can do."
Jesus knew He was going to die.
He told His disciples so in John 13:33.
Then, to those troubled hearts
He gave words of comfort and hope
in telling them that through Himself there is life
and reunion in the Father's house.

Death is not a friend.
Paul names it correctly. It is the last great enemy.
Jesus saw it that way.
Mark says that, in Gethsemane's garden,
Jesus was greatly distressed and troubled
at the prospect of death.
He asked that the cup might pass from Him (14:33, 36).
It was not the pain, but the realization
that He would be in the hands of the enemy,
which troubled Him.
And so He cried out at the cross
of His "forsakenness"
as He grappled with the enemy.

I have watched many people die
in my twenty years as a minister.
And while we are glad that suffering is over
and that they are now "face to face with Christ their Saviour,"
suffering and death are the enemy's doing.

I sat by as Lindon died.
He accepted death.
He was honest about it.
He knew the hope beyond.
But he struggled to stay awake. I shall never forget that.
I saw something alien and foreign,
the work of the enemy, in that hospital room.

Before we get to the Father's house,
we face the enemy.

Another fact that validates the promise of Jesus
is that our hope is in His resurrection and ours.
The sting of death is taken away in the resurrection.
The victory of the grave
is negated in the resurrection.

Not many hours before Lindon died
I prayed with him for grace and strength
for that lonely battle.
He was glad we were there.
As Jesus wanted people with Him in Gethsemane
before His death,
so no one wants to die alone.
He asked Nancy and Lloyd to play Scrabble
so that he would hear people nearby.

I talked awhile
and asked him what sermons he had left in his series
on the Apostles' Creed.
He fought to think
because the thought process was slowly ebbing.
He said: "The Forgiveness of Sins and The Resurrection
of the Body" and "The Life Everlasting."
And his voice rose stronger on the term,
"the resurrection of the body."

This is where we win.
It was at His resurrection
where Jesus beat Satan on his own home field.
He suffered death.
He was in the hands of the enemy.
He entered the realm of the enemy and conquered him there.
God raised Jesus from the dead!
Death could not hold Him.
And He became the first fruits of them that slept (1 Corinthians 15:20).

On resurrection day,
we will be called forth as spiritual bodies
set free from the power of evil,
and we will live upon the new, redeemed earth.
Though we must wait till that day,
it is our sure hope.

I have consciously walked some years now with death.
I have measured his power.
I know he is my enemy.
But words cannot tell you how meaningful
it is to know that death is defeated.
Surely we live in "the already but not yet,"
but it is enough to know
that Satan has lost decisively.
And the covenant God, the God who makes
and keeps promises,
says that he will be cast into a lake of fire
on the great day!
O death, now where is thy sting!
O grave, now where is thy victory!

We shall live in the Father's house—
not as immortal souls, but as spiritual bodies—
resurrected from the dead.

What is it like?
No one describes it well.
Paul said that no eye has seen, no ear heard,
no heart conceived,
what God has prepared for those who love him (1 Corinthians 2:9).
Bunyan's Pilgrim, when he came within sight of the eternal city,
tried to look at it through his glass,
but his hand shook so that he could not clearly see.

We do have some descriptions.
Heaven is described in terms of space, ruled over by God.

John says heaven is the Father's house.
Revelation speaks of a great city,
four square,
and the writer of Hebrews calls it a country,
a commonwealth.
The common denominator of all of these descriptions
is that heaven belongs to God.

Heaven is described in terms of its inhabitants.
Little children shall be there
beholding the face of the Father.
Publicans, harlots, sinners,
forgiven through the atonement of the cross, shall be there.
Martyrs who died for the most holy faith
will inhabit that land.
Someone has said that these things will surprise us in heaven:
those who are there,
those who are not there,
and that we are there.

Heaven is described in terms of values.
There is a permanency about it,
for thieves cannot break in and steal.
Again, there is eternality:
"The things which are not seen are eternal" (2 Corinthians 4:18).
"The fountain of the water of life" (Revelation 21:6, KJV)
quenching our thirst,
speaks of the satisfaction found finally in heaven.

Heaven is described in terms of its blessings.
In relation to God,
we will hear His "well done,
thou good and faithful servant: . . .
enter thou into the joy of thy lord" (Matthew 25:21, KJV).
In relation to loved ones,
1 Thessalonians 4 takes for granted
that we shall know one another and there will be reunion.

The beautiful description of Revelation 21
says that there will be relief from suffering
and rest from the oppressive labors of existence.

But there is an understanding of heaven we talk little about.
Heaven is a place of progress.
We will continue to grow.

While there are few chapters and verses
to which we can point,
it seems to me that the whole tenor of Scripture
is that of progress in God's expanding cosmos.
We will continue what we were programmed by God to be,
and what, in Christ, we have begun on earth.
I think heaven is a journey of many stages,
during which a development of ourselves goes on.

In our being, our self, our personality,
we will continue on,
even though now clothed, as Paul says,
with a new resurrection or "spiritual" body.
We will not be victims of cut-off growth.
The infant who has died will grow up over there.
Those for whom our fallen sinful creation
has dealt such cruel blows
will be unfettered there.
The lame shall walk and the blind shall see!
Those cut off in the prime of life
shall continue to become what they are programmed to be.

There will be continuing service and the sharpening of gifts.
We will not retire in heaven.
We will learn to do things we need to do.
Revelation 22:3, "And His bond-servants shall serve Him."

Heaven is a society. There is division of labor.
We will serve one another joyfully.
If Jesus in His resurrection body
ate in the upper room and on the road to Emmaus,

perhaps we will have to work to eat.
But it will not be in the sweat of our brow,
nor will the ground bear thorns and thistles.
Nor will we ever face the demeaning monotony
of the assembly line.

There will be continual progression of knowledge
as described in 1 Corinthians 13:12:

> For now we see in a mirror dimly, but then face to face;
> Now I know in part, but then I shall know fully just as I also
> have been fully known.

It is unlikely that it will happen all at once.
But we shall understand more fully.
We will understand why.

We will understand how everything relates,
how all knowledge fits together,
a comprehensive understanding of all things.
The pieces—science, arts, letters—will fit together.
That will be a delightful eternity of study for some.

In this life we live, learn, grow, and serve the Master.
Death will not change that.
For life will be a continuing process
then, unfettered from the enemy of our souls
and the effects of the Fall.

On the day we hear the trumpet in the morning,
Jesus, who said, "I will come again,
and receive you to Myself" (John 14:3),
will come back for us.

We will meet a lot of people that day
in a joyous community of life.
We will meet a man with a warm smile,
a preacher with a sense of humor
and a deep thirst for understanding.

Like as not, you will find him studying,
preaching, or—Bible in hand—
disputing with Paul
over some particularly enigmatic passage.

That will be Lindon Karo:
faithful pastor,
serious student of the Word,
preacher extraordinary,
man of God.

Peace be to the memory of that man!

* * *

That night, as I recorded in my diary the events of the day, I added, "Lin did leave in a blaze of glory!"